Tortilla
Chronicles

TORTILLA CHRONICLES

Growing Up in Santa Fe

MARIE ROMERO CASH

University of New Mexico Press
ALBUQUERQUE

12 11 10 09 08 07   1 2 3 4 5 6

Library of Congress Cataloging-in-Publication Data

Cash, Marie Romero.
  Tortilla chronicles : growing up in Santa Fe /
Marie Romero Cash.
      p. cm.
  ISBN-13: 978-0-8263-3912-6 (cloth : alk. paper)
  1. Cash, Marie Romero. 2. Folk artists—New Mexico—
Santa Fe—Biography. I. Title.
  NK839.C37C37 2007
  709.2—dc22
  [B] 7862537

                                    2006100669

Book design and composition by Damien Shay
Body type is Trump Mediaeval 10/14
Display is Bureau Eagle Book and Fajita

Contents

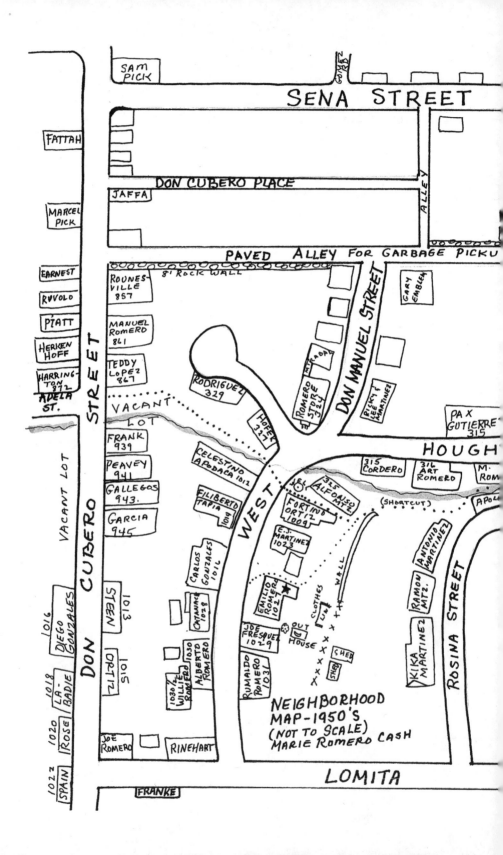

NEIGHBORHOOD
MAP—1950'S
(NOT TO SCALE)
MARIE ROMERO CASH

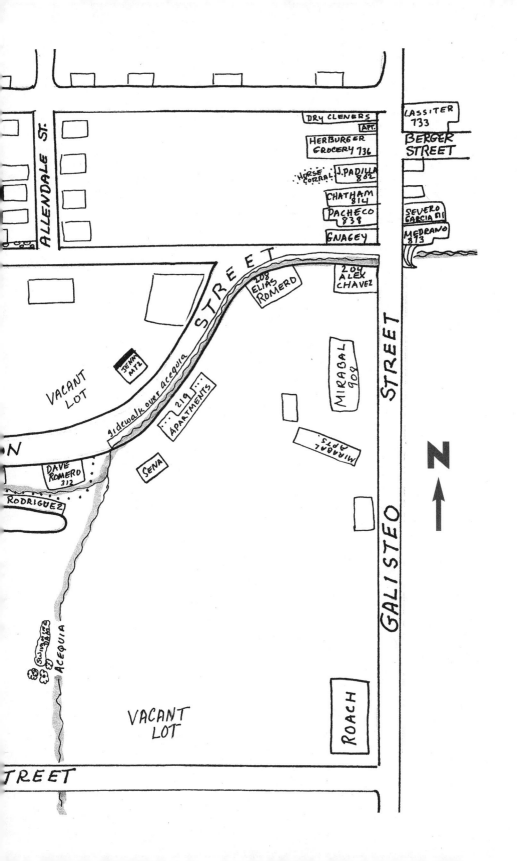

Prologue

I have lived in Santa Fe most of my life. I have come to believe that Santa Fe *is* my family. I have left several times and greeted with open arms when I returned. I belong here. In the years I was away from home, Mother sent me care packages—a dozen tortillas, a couple of jars of red chile, and a box of *biscochitos*. All I had to do was buy a block of cheddar cheese, and voila, a lip-smacking enchilada dinner graced my kitchen table. The places I lived were full of culture...theirs, not mine. Florida didn't have my food or music, and the same held true in Arizona. In 1973 I was divorced with three children, so it was natural to return home to my family ties. Santa Fe represented not only my beginnings, but also the middle and most likely the end. All my major life relationships have developed in Santa Fe, and the roots of my life here go deep. I learned my life lessons here, and the culture was etched in my soul. When I lived in other places, Santa Fe always pulled at me. It was only here that I felt the air wrap itself around me like a flannel blanket. I was safe and secure because I was in the only place I could truly call home. In addition, my six brothers and sisters all lived here.

Walking east on San Francisco Street toward the downtown plaza one hot, muggy summer afternoon in 1996, I realized how

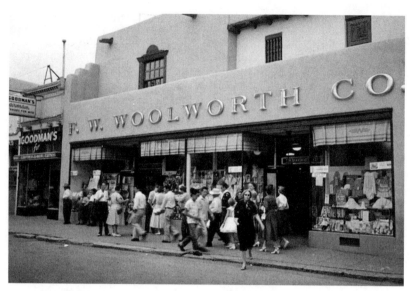

Downtown Santa Fe, 1955. Photo courtesy Joseph E. Valdes.

much everything in Santa Fe had changed. I tried to conjure up images of store facades from the 1950s: the Mayflower Café, Capitol Pharmacy, Franklin's Department Store, Moore's Men's Store, and Leed's Shoe Store. It was hard to believe they no longer existed. I turned around at St. Francis Cathedral, our historic parish church in the heart of the city, and decided to walk back down the street. Surely I was wrong. Well, I was ... but only slightly. The only remaining vestiges of that era were the historic Fred Harvey La Fonda Hotel, built in 1922, and the equally old Camera Shop across the street. I gazed down the block and noticed that other old familiar businesses were missing: La Tienda, The Guarantee, Sears, and Bell's—every building replaced by a trendy gallery, gift shop, clothing store, ice cream parlor, or restaurant.

Down near the west end of San Francisco Street stood the only other holdout, the Lensic Theater, and it was soon to undergo extensive renovation. The Lensic renovation would not only provide necessary restoration to the interior, but the process would transform the building into a performing arts center, and probably leave room for other additions, perhaps a hotel. (Santa Fe

Lensic Theater. Photo courtesy Karl Eschenbach.

is infamous for allowing unplanned structures to be built long after the city fathers have approved the original concept.)

The Lensic was built in 1931 by the Salmon-Greer family. It was the finest theater in the Southwest, providing wealthy Santa Feans with the opportunity to see such great Hollywood stage and screen stars as Rita Hayworth, Rudy Vallee, Errol Flynn, Olivia de Havilland, and Judy Garland. Designed by the famed Boller Brothers of Kansas City, it captured the imaginations of all with its romantic and exotic Moorish architecture and motifs. The interior of the building was plush and glamorous, with colorful murals painted on the walls. The seats were soft and velvety, and the floors were covered with intricately designed deep pile carpet in colors worthy of the Taj Mahal. Even the bathroom walls were lined with gleaming tile and floor-length mirrors.

Bona fide natives who recalled Santa Fe's early history didn't like the change in the city's landscape, as in 1986 when the Eldorado Hotel, a half block from the Lensic, bolted into the blue expanse of Santa Fe sky, blocking views for miles around. A seven-level, 1,800-room building wasn't much in large cities across the United States, but in Santa Fe it was monolithic in proportion to other buildings on the plaza. Just the excavation of the huge underground parking lot was amazing to watch. The hotel was built on a large corner lot of prime Santa Fe real estate that for decades had housed Big Jo Lumber, a locally owned store where one could purchase lumber, hardware, and other building materials. (This immense structure likely paved the way for eventual transformation of the plaza area.)

Looking around the bustling plaza, the 1950s seemed like a lifetime away. My father, Emilio Rodríguez Romero, was eighty-six years old and experiencing short bursts of memory loss. Many times he said, "Write this down...it's important," and he'd relate some tidbit about his childhood. He was in frail condition, no longer six foot tall and 240 pounds, but closer to 180 and slowly dwindling. "I don't know what I ever did to deserve this punishment," he complained as he struggled to move from his wheelchair to the bed in the dimly lit bedroom he and my mother had occupied for more than six decades. But we both knew he had lived a prosperous, long life, even though he struggled to maintain his dignity as he attempted to stand without assistance on legs that no longer cooperated. This loss of mobility crept up slowly over the years. For whatever reason, the nerve bundles in his spine no longer carried the "walk" message from the brain. No reasonable medical explanation was ever given, but some of us felt it had been caused by some type of exposure to radioactivity at his job in Los Alamos. In recent years some of his old coworkers had been diagnosed with various ailments relating to their employment there, but Dad never wanted to pursue this.

These days Dad was sentimental to the core. An old Spanish song like "Flor de las Flores" would spark a memory long forgotten and tears would run unashamedly down his cheeks, and the sadness of the moment pierced me to the bone. He often told me how proud he was of his heritage, of having been born in Santa Fe to parents of Spanish descent whose roots in New Mexico were centuries deep. He never forgot all the rituals and traditions that shaped him during childhood. Every time I hear a chorus of "Las Mañanitas," tears well in my eyes, too, as the haunting melody transports me to another time.

Except for weekends, Dad wore khaki work pants and shirts, with steel-toed leather work shoes. A hardworking man, he learned his work ethic at an early age. After retiring from Zia Company in Los Alamos in the early seventies, he and Mother devoted their days to handcrafting practical and decorative items out of tin, including mirror frames, switchplates, and Kleenex box covers. Married for more than sixty years, they worked together in their kitchen workshop, beginning their workday after breakfast and finishing up at four o'clock. Mom would then clear off the table and Dad would unscrew the top from a cold bottle of Budweiser. He read *The Santa Fe New Mexican* and she prepared dinner.

For more than thirty years at this same table, they fashioned thousands of tin boxes, sconces, *nichos*, and candleholders. Each day as I walked up their driveway, a short block from my house around the corner, I could hear the steady sound of dueling hammers against handmade steel-stamping tools as they tapped out intricate designs on sheets of tin. Over the years as their small cottage industry developed, they became nationally known for their work, but their fame never affected the way they conducted business. People from all walks of life visited the house on Houghton Street to buy items for their gift shops or homes. Contractors ordered thousands of light switch covers for the Santa Fe–style homes they were building. My parents kept prices reasonable because Dad believed, "You'll never go broke making a small profit." He said this often, since he thought the middleman should also make a profit. On a daily basis he cut out patterns from tin and marked the lines on them for design. At first Mom only stamped small dots around the edges, but later she graduated to completing pieces by herself. Dad then stamped out large, circular flower patterns, after which Mom bent the edges before he soldered the pieces together. All the while, the delicate strains of corridos (Mexican ballads) coming from the radio could be heard in the background.

I spent many hours talking to my parents about their lives in early Santa Fe. I grew up on West Houghton Street and now lived around the corner from my old neighborhood, so I spent a lot of time with them. As my father approached his death in early

April of 1997, I sat next to his bed and tried to feed him small spoonfuls of atole, reminding him that he needed to keep up his strength. But I believe he knew he was dying and was looking for a way to break the news to me. He didn't want to be alone, and many times I stayed until he fell asleep. He told me how much he had loved my mother all through the years, and that he knew he hadn't been the best of fathers, but he had done the best he could. He said he loved all his children, and I couldn't hold back the tears as he told me how much he had loved and appreciated me, that I had always been his "favorite." As a child, when the boys were off doing something else, I was the one who went fishing and rock hounding with him. It was a conversation I wished we'd had twenty years earlier when I was struggling to make sense of life and relationships, but I was heartened to finally hear his words, knowing they'd been long in coming.

My parents were never able to express their feelings, toward us or each other, although we never questioned their love. Over the past fifty-something years, I imagine many things went unsaid. Anger was expressed far more easily than love. My dad died, I believe, longing to make amends for his mistakes as a parent, but happy that at least with me he had shared forgiveness. Immediately after his death, our family arrived, and we gathered around him and prayed, hoping his journey toward heaven would be far easier than his life on earth had been. He died during Holy Week and was buried at Rosario Cemetery on Easter Monday.

Following his death, I had a great void in my life. During Dad's final months, Mother was exhibiting signs of the early stages of Alzheimer's disease, and at the time of his death, she, too, was with us only in spirit. At the age of fifty-eight, I was in the process of beginning my studies at the University of New Mexico toward a master's degree. I was the recipient of a Javits Fellowship and excited about the coming months and the fulfillment of my life's dream. Three days a week I traveled to Albuquerque to attend classes, and then headed over to the elder care facility where she spent her last days. It was difficult to watch the progression of this insidious disease as it slowly dimmed the sparkle in her eyes in the ensuing months. My schedule proved to be a difficult one, and I withdrew from school to devote more time to being with Mother, knowing her time on earth was limited.

The evening before she died in February of 2001, a small, gray bird perched on the leafless apricot tree outside my bedroom window. I found it odd that the bird wouldn't fly away and figured it had lost its way. I believed that maybe this wonderful creature was a messenger, an omen sent from another universe, and this thought made me smile just as I was dropping off to sleep. My sister Rosalie called in the middle of the night to tell me the news of Mom's death, and we prayed for her over the phone, thankful that she had died peacefully in her sleep. With my mother's passing, it was as though my life links had been broken, as though she was the end of the chain that connected me to the past. She was the one I had hoped to travel with; I wanted to show her the wonders of the world, to watch her excitement as she looked out from the window of an airplane to see the broad expanse of the earth below. There would be no more visits to the nursing home in Albuquerque, driving sixty miles and bringing small, insignificant trinkets or gifts, much like we did as children. In her childlike state, she relished those shiny bracelets and a baby doll that talked when a button was pressed on its stomach. My sisters and I spent many visits painting her fingernails in bright reds and pinks, much to her delight, the fingernails that had rarely been painted due to the beating they took from pounding on the tin for so many years. Growing up I thought my parents would always be here to guide us, Dad with his subtle humor and Mom with her never-ending prayers.

Months before my mother died, we sold the family home to provide professional care for her, and although the house on Houghton Street is no longer in the family, the memories linger. In my mind I can still walk from the living room to the kitchen and hear the hammers' incessant pounding against tin, noisy but music to my ears. Other times I can smell the heady aroma of freshly made tortillas and green chile stew. And, if I try really hard, the aromatic anise smell of biscochitos comes crashing through my senses.

At Mom's funeral, our cousin and next-door neighbor E. J. "Junior," Martínez said in his eulogy, "When Tía Senaida made tortillas, the aroma would immediately draw us all to their kitchen door to see if Jimmy could come out and play. As we stood outside the old wooden screen door, we knew she would offer us a tortilla. Sometimes they were plain, sometimes with jelly, and sometimes with the best green chile we ever tasted."

Like so much of Santa Fe, Mom's old house has changed completely, but if she could see it, she'd be proud. It's now everything she ever wanted her home to be. The floor plan is vastly different: the kitchen where they worked for so many years is now a family room, with French doors opening out to a walled garden that extends to the area where the clotheslines once stood. The *cuartito*, the old storage room then makeshift bedroom, is now the kitchen. The old master bedroom is now a hallway, and the aluminum windows have all been replaced, but the hardwood floors still glisten. Even the yard is different. The seventy-year-old apple tree planted in the front yard when my sister Anita was born had recently been shattered by lightning; the equally old apricot tree and most of the lilac bushes have had to be trimmed. An immense flower garden pushes against the front wall, as though Mother had personally overseen the selection of plants, and a growth of ivy covers most of the wall. How could the new owners have known this same ivy covered our front porch in the early years? Even part of the old *percha* (clothesline) was embedded near the lilac bush, and the old, yellow kitchen window frames decorate the patio. The sunken garden pays tribute to my parents' great love of trees and flowers, and the genuine warmth of the house still remains. The freshly plastered front porch beckons one to come and sit, the fireplace still stands in the center of the former living room, and as I imagine my hands warmed by a roaring blaze on a winter night, I feel memories returning unbidden: memories of growing up in Santa Fe in the 1950s.

Introduction

EARLY SANTA FE AND MY NEIGHBORHOOD

A h, Santa Fe...when I think about my home I feel a steady warmth in my heart kindled by memories of growing up in a town with dusty roads, friendly smiling people, and the bluest of azure skies in the world. *Who says you can't come home?*

It's hard to imagine Santa Fe back then, without four-lane traffic, bypasses, St. Francis Drive, Paseo de Peralta, and the saturation of speed bumps, stop signs, and traffic lights at every corner; without the hundreds of residential neighborhoods and the throngs of tourists, McDonald's, Taco Bell, Pizza Hut, art galleries, and shopping malls. In the 1950s Cerrillos Road was the main street in and out of town. Downtown Santa Fe consisted mostly of businesses owned and operated by locals. There were no shopping malls. For us, the city ended just past Ingram's Drive-In, with the Yucca Drive-In Theater and Ly'n'Bragg Truck Stop a few miles south up the road. Albuquerque was a million miles away. If so inclined, you could take a leisurely drive north

1

East San Francisco Street, 1950s. Photo courtesy the Fray Angélico
Chávez History Library.

up the Old Taos Highway or Bishop's Lodge Road, areas not yet
populated by thousands of Santa Fe–style homes. We had large
open spaces, and we could look out our back doors and see for
miles in every direction. No other streets existed south of the
dirt road that intersected where West Houghton Street ended at
a then-unoccupied Lomita Street. To the west we could see all
the way to Cerrillos Road and the State Penitentiary.

Our neighborhood was called La Loma, the hill. We had an
endless expanse of playground, with piñon trees, tall grasses,
and good old brown earth. On the outskirts the town was lined
with bars, liquor stores, gas stations, pharmacies, barbershops,
and a platoon of lawyers to serve the community, along with a
number of doctors and dentists. We even had a Chinese restaurant, the New Canton Café, a place where the cuisine was so foreign to us that we settled for looking curiously through the
windows, watching people eat rice with small sticks.

I remember waking up to bursts of color draping the landscape like a well-worn kaleidoscope in the fall and snuggling
under warm, quilted covers in the winter, as the surrounding

jagged Sangre de Cristo Mountains wore blankets of snow like layers of white frosting. And when the sun was at its highest around midday, its shimmering reflection was hypnotic. Then there was summertime, and the living was easy...enjoyably mild days, rarely above eighty degrees, cooled by undulating mountain breezes and impromptu rain showers...the fields and arroyos covered with varying shades of yellow daisies and purple lilacs, and later on as the days dipped toward midsummer, with long, green stalks of multicolored hollyhocks. Like clockwork, every mid-September for many years Dad said, "When you see those little yellow wildflowers growing all over the place, it's a sure sign that summer is over." And sure enough, every late September when I see them, I know summer has come to an end.

The roads in and around Santa Fe were mainly dirt, except for those around the historic plaza, which were brick and cement. Back then, few of the houses were plastered but made from plain adobe blocks and mud; there were no walls or fences surrounding the yards, no grass, no sidewalks, no pavement. Horny toads populated areas between rocks and plants. Not everyone owned a car, everything was centrally located, and Santa Fe was more like a large village than a small town. Founded in 1610 and resettled in 1692, Santa Fe was built around a beautiful central plaza now filled with huge pine trees intermingled with elms, grassy patches, and metal benches, bordered by a myriad of downtown shops, hotels, and cafés and the historic Palace of the Governors, where dozens of Native Americans spend their days selling jewelry, pottery, and weavings.

Growing up, there was a grassy park next to the Santa Fe River that ran along the length of Alameda Street and traversed west. Children of all ages built dams and walked barefoot through the riverbed before the summer rains swelled the aquifers. A midsummer rush of bubbling water delighted the more daring who proudly stood in the middle of the river as the water pushed past their bare legs. Even Rosario Cemetery at the north end of town was beautifully maintained. In those days families lovingly placed plastic flowers, candles, and mementos on the graves of their loved ones. The slightest breeze would spin colorful plastic pinwheels left in the children's section by grieving parents. Neighborhood grocery stores still existed, mom-and-pop operations where you could stop for a Popsicle or a candy bar after school, or run down the street for a loaf of bread before lunch.

West Houghton Street was about a mile south of downtown in an area referred to as South Capitol. It was a neighborhood of Spanish* families, many of whom were related by degrees and most of whom had been born in the neighborhood. As a young girl I wondered why our street was named after an Anglo, since Houghton Street was surrounded on all sides by streets with Spanish names: Don Cubero, Don Manuel, Don Diego, Don Gaspar, and Don Fernando, and all the residents of the street had Spanish surnames. As an adult, I discovered our street was named after Joab Houghton, New Mexico's supreme court chief justice in the 1840s. He had a long and colorful history, both in politics and in business. He controlled most of the stone quarries around Santa Fe and built the State Penitentiary and the Federal Building downtown. In addition, he was a friend of Governor Charles Bent, who was killed in the Taos Revolt of 1847.

In the 1860s Houghton Street and the surrounding area were part of a land grant known as the Mesita de Juana Lopez grant. Through a quiet title suit, Houghton came into possession of a huge portion of property stretching from Cerrillos Road to the Old Pecos Trail. Years later, the Houghton holdings passed from his heirs to Benito Ortíz and his wife Clemencia, as heirs of Encarnación Lujan, and then parts of it to my father's family in 1917. Don Canuto Romero (no relation, and for whom Don Canuto Street a short distance west was named) owned the surrounding property. Around the turn of the century, Don Benito began to develop our street and built his house (now numbered 1028). His original intention was to face the street west, toward Cerrillos Road, so he built the house facing in that direction, but

* I have used the term "Spanish" throughout this book, as it is the term we used when referring to ourselves while growing up. I realize there are more modern words in use such as "Hispanic," "Hispano," "Nuevomexicano," "Chicano," etc., but "Spanish" is the word I am most comfortable with.

later homebuilders didn't follow his example. Situated across from my parents' house, it is the only structure with the porch facing the backyard and the back door facing the street. This house and the small house behind it (both later owned by the Catanach family) were the oldest houses in the neighborhood. To the north of Houghton Street, which adjoins Don Manuel Street (named in 1903 for Manuel P. Romero), was an old Territorial–style house, which appears to predate the houses on West Houghton. The front of the original house is on Don Manuel and the adjacent house with a common room wall is on West Houghton. Doña Rosarito Ortíz owned this house and later sold it to the Mirabal family. The 1930s addition fronting Houghton Street would house a small grocery store. Down the gravel driveway next to it is an old two-room adobe house originally owned by Doña Kika Lechúga, who was already up in years in the 1930s. It consisted of two rooms next to an old woodshed that her son Chéne filled with wood brought on mules, which he cut and delivered to the various neighbors for their woodstoves. Each burro-load sold for fifty cents and pieces were cut to fit the stove. Doña Kika's husband Ascencíon sold the house to their daughter Eloisa Rodríguez, who with her husband and later as a widow raised a large family. The small house in front was purchased by Mabel Hofer, who lived there only a short time and then rented it out. My aunt Mela Frésquez and her husband Joe lived there when they were newly married in the mid-1930s, before their house at 1029 West Houghton was built.

Grandma and Grandpa Romero bought a large plot of land on the west side of the street in 1917, built their house by 1918, and moved from 224 Hickox Street, where my father, Aunt Mela, and Uncle Rumaldo were born. Uncles Willie and Rudy were born at 1030 West Houghton. My grandmother's sister Josefita and her husband Fortino Ortíz later bought property on the north side of the street and hired Don Merejildo to build their house early in the 1920s. In 1930 my father bought a good chunk of the east side of the street with money he saved. When our house was built, only Don Canuto's house at 1028, Tío Fortino's house, and my grandparents' house occupied our neighborhood. During the 1930s, five members of my grandmother's extended family built houses in the surrounding area. On the plot of land to the east of our house, another Martínez family from the village of Ojo de la Vaca near Pecos arrived during the 1920s by a horse-drawn carriage, with wagons filled with all their belongings, to build their house on land given to them by Encarnación Lujan some years before his death. Although they were not related to us, Prima Kíka and her four children became part of the closely knit neighborhood. Their three-room adobe house had the only pitched roof in the area, and it fronted on San Isabel Street, parallel to West Houghton Street.

As more houses sprung up in the neighborhood, we grew up encircled by grandparents, uncles, aunts, and cousins. It was the best life had to offer.

Chapter One

IT'S ALL RELATIVE

My Mother and Her Family

Senaida Ortega was a woman of small stature, but great of heart. She was born in Cañoncito, a small village southwest of Santa Fe on July 18, 1909, the youngest of five children, two boys and three girls: Brigida, Genaro, Arturo, Sally, and Senaida.

When she was a young woman being courted by my father, she stood at a spunky five foot two and had black hair and hazel green eyes. Mom's skin was light, and her thick eyebrows framed her eyes. She wore just a little makeup, a light powder and lipstick. She dressed in the style of the day, not in expensive clothes, but nicely fitted dresses with hems a few inches below the knee. The shoes were mid-heel with open toes. Her hair was styled in a mid-length bob, but not too short, parted on the left side with waves closely framing her face. As her hair grew, she wore it pinned back above her head. She had a shy smile that made you want to reach out and hug her.

Emilio R. Romero and
Senaida Ortega, 1929.

Mother never wasted any time; in fact, she was usually a whirlwind of activity. She cooked, sewed, mended socks, cleaned, and generally cared for all of us. She had a gentle spirit and seemed to be blessed with endless strength. She attended school only through sixth grade and beamed with pride as we advanced from grade to grade. She never raised her voice, and if we ever brought her to tears, we would have felt bad, so mostly we tried to be obedient and respectful children.

She had an expression for everything. When people were obstinate or rude, out of their hearing she would say, "*Que Dios lo tenga de una oreja,*" which meant, "May God have him by one ear." For the worst conduct and most serious or character offenses, she would intone, "*Que se muera con un ratón en la boca,*" which meant, "May he die with a rat in his mouth." These two sayings would evoke gales of laughter from us as we tried to visualize such an event. *Malacacha* was a word she used for people who were particularly rude.

As a child, she learned to crochet by using a sewing needle and a piece of string unwound from a flour sack. She became adept at creating doilies long before she was introduced to a crochet hook early in her marriage. Most of the women in our community crocheted. I recall seeing heavily starched, ruffled doilies scattered on furniture in every home around the neighborhood and often wondered if these women were engaged in a competition to see who could create the most beautiful ones. Doilies sprouted everywhere: under lamps, statues, and candy dishes (for those who had candy). When my mother mastered a crochet hook, the formerly small doilies became big doilies, and the big doilies became tablecloths, pillow covers, and even dresses and hats for small plastic dolls. Mother developed patterns by counting the numbers of stitches and rows required. She couldn't understand the complicated printed instructions that came with the rolls of multicolored crochet thread and patterns. I patiently read them to her until she memorized them. It was a strange language: "2sc ten times followed by 1tc and 5dc." Without knowing it, she'd been doing it correctly for years.

Mother never learned how to drive. Dad tried to teach her only once when they were newlyweds, but the outing turned into a disaster. After pulling out of the driveway and onto the dirt road in his Model-T Ford, Dad stopped the car and began the lesson. After a few blocks of uneventful driving, he had her turn onto Galisteo Street and head home to West Houghton Street, where she expertly turned right and continued up the small hill. There was a large boulder sitting in the middle of the street, and since he didn't tell her to avoid it, she ran right into it and broke the axle of the car. Because of this, she never attempted to drive again, and he never attempted to teach her.

My mother's parents, Santiago Ortega and Inés García, married in 1897 in Santa Fe. When Mother was a child, the family moved to a small rural community, Ojo de la Vaca (Cow Springs), near the village of Pecos about twenty-five miles east of Santa Fe in San Miguel County. New Mexico became part of the United States in 1912, thereby enabling residents to apply under the

Santiago and Inés Ortega,
Ojo de La Vaca, NM, 1920.

Homestead Act to receive 160 acres of land in various commu-
nities in New Mexico. My grandfather Santiago, along with
many of his relatives, applied for and received a homestead,
some families sharing the acreage between them. By the end of
the summer the family was living in Ojo with fifty other families, which were all related in some way, while their house was
under construction. More than a hundred people formed the
community, and many houses were needed. Each family shared
the task, hoping to finish before the winter snows came. Most of
the families were unprepared for the harsh winters, with temperatures colder than most places in New Mexico. The snow fell
in heaps, creating layer upon layer until the drifts covered everything in sight. Sometimes the livestock did not survive. Mother
recalled, "Can you imagine seeing an animal completely frozen
in its tracks, still covered with snow? Papá Santiago explained
that it was a peaceful death; that the animal didn't suffer." Were
it not for wisps of smoke coming from the chimneys, there

Senaida Ortega,
First Holy Communion,
Ojo de la Vaca, 1916.

would be little evidence of life in this community. After each heavy snow the boys in the family shoveled a path to the school and church, and life continued as usual.

My maternal grandparents' house was L-shaped with three rooms built of adobes, and every room had a window. They shared an outdoor bathroom with neighbors in the immediate area. It was the women's task to mud-plaster the house inside and out, which they did every few years. The floors were mud that had been patiently smoothed with water and left to dry. The rock-hard floors shone like glass. Each day the walls and floors were dusted with a rabbit hide. The interior walls were sparsely decorated, usually with religious prints. A nearby well belonging to Primo Patricio García, the town carpenter, provided water for the family.

At the edge of the community was a *tendejón*, a small store primarily for necessities. Each month the family traveled about ten miles to nearby Lamy, a railroad town, to shop for larger

items. Everyone owned a wagon pulled by a horse or mule. Tío
José owned the only automobile, and every so often he would go
from house to house making a list of all his neighbors' needs,
then make the trip to Lamy accompanied by as many children as
could fit in the car. Everyone had a charge account at the country store, and when cattle were sold in the spring, the store-
keeper was always the first to be paid.

Mother recalled Santiago Ortega as a kind and gentle father.
An avid hunter, he provided deer, rabbit, and wild turkeys for the
family. He earned most of his income as a sheepherder, which
took him away from the family for long periods of time. He came
home in the summer after shearing the sheep and returned to the
pasture in the winter. Everyone in the community was self-
employed, raising farm animals and planting crops of onions,
peas, *frijol*, *melón*, *calabazas*, and watermelons that grew to be
two feet long, irrigated only by rain. The men grew crops of
punché, large tobacco leaves for hand-rolled cigarettes. Leading up
to 1918, the area experienced a severe drought, eliminating plants
and gardens. It became more difficult to feed the family, though
Santiago continued to fish and hunt. Mother recalled they sometimes ate just one meal a day—a tortilla with a thin gravy made
from meat stock, flour, and water. They kept only a few animals,
as food for them was also scarce. Hundreds of rabbits raised by
neighboring relatives soon became thin and sickly. My mother
and her sister Sally were sent out in the blistering summer sun to
search for cactus and other plants to feed the remaining two cows
and goats. They hurried along to avoid snakes, but more so to
avoid La Llorona (a legendary bogeywoman from northern New
Mexico who is said to haunt arroyos searching for unruly kids to
terrorize). They were afraid she was lurking around the arroyos,
waiting to kidnap them and take them far away. When they
encountered a clump of cactus, with a small, makeshift shovel
and their left hands wrapped in many layers of flour sack cloth,
they scooped the cactus into another cloth bag and carried it
home. The chunks of cactus were fed to the goats, since the cows
were hesitant to partake of these spiny delicacies.

Grandma Inés García was born in 1880 in Santa Fe. As a
married woman, she kept the house clean, tended to the garden,

and raised the children. Mother recalls that she was energetic and industrious as a housewife. She taught the children to milk the cows each morning and to separate the cream to make cheese, and to celebrate the Christmas holidays by making decorations from homegrown popcorn.

Grandma Inés taught her children to believe in God and walked with them to the monthly Mass held in the small one-room chapel that had been built by Primo Patricio on a nearby hillside. Since the priest came only once a month to say Mass, Mother recalled, "Everyone would get in line to say their confession, including neighbors from the towns around us. There was no real confessional. Just some sheets draped over boards in the corner of the room. He couldn't make another trip, so we'd have a short Mass right after confession. Then he'd get back into his horse-drawn wagon and go back to Pecos."

Clothing was handmade, and Inés relied on her seamstress cousins for handed-down dresses they copied from the Sears catalog for Mother and her two sisters. Sunday outfits were catalog-bought, usually handed down by a relative in Santa Fe who had access to more clothing than she knew what to do with. The dresses were high-necked, long-sleeved cotton with belted skirts worn over dark stockings. Shoes were purchased only when one pair was no longer usable and if the family could afford it. In the winter, warm hats were made from sheepskin. There were no store-bought dolls available. Rag dolls were made from cotton cloth purchased at the store and filled with straw. Inés taught the girls to embroider, and they easily applied eyes and mouths to their new dolls. Even rabbit skins were filled with straw and the sides sewn up. These became furry stuffed animals for children. There was always a ball for the boys to toss around and frayed cloth sacks filled with marbles.

As if the drought had not been enough to test the villagers' endurance, the influenza epidemic of 1918 transformed the small community into a ghost town. Mother recalled, *"Todos estaban enfermos*, everyone was sick. There was nobody to even cook meals or to dig the graves." The virulent and debilitating illness spread like wildfire through one region, and Mother thought it was because everyone drank the same water. Many

Sally and Senaida Ortega,
Ojo de la Vaca, 1921.

people died within a week of the outbreak. Mom's Primo
Patricio, *el papá de prima Kika*, made the caskets, but after a
while they ran out of lumber and simply buried the people along
with their sheets and blankets on top of each other in quickly
dug graves. When the epidemic ended, Mother recalled that
there was silence...not even a dog barked. All the people she
had known most of her life, her neighbors, relatives, and friends,
were gone in less than a month. Tía Nicolasa and her entire family died. And as was her nature, Mom had a story about how the
influenza epidemic ended when a stranger came to town. She
recalled, "*Me acuerdo poquito, un hombre vestido en negro
venía todo el camino.* We could see him on the horizon, all
dressed in black, carrying some sort of *maleta*, or valise, and he
began to visit all of the houses, *y les daba una medicina, o no
sé qué*, and at each house the inhabitants drank this medicine,
or at least they thought it was medicine. Nobody actually saw

the mysterious substance, *y todos sanaban*, but no matter, they all got well."

In the summer of 2002, Mother's ninety-four-year-old cousin Isabel García de Valdez recalled the same incident. "It was terrible, half the people died, complete families. We were fortunate to lose no one in our area. A doctor from Santa Fe came, dressed in blue, like a Marine. He wore a face mask. Don't worry, he said, I come from the government. Open all the windows and doors, don't get wet or chilled. He left medicine for everyone to drink. They were large plastic gallons with red liquid left at all the houses. The illness lasted really long—nobody could eat— lots of youngsters were affected, but none of the old folks in our family. We took care of everyone, because they were all weak. Eventually with great effort, we were able to kill a chicken, hang it on the door, and defeather it. My tío cooked it with a lot of broth. It was the first food most were able to digest. I thanked the Lord that we lost no one."

Grandpa Santiago died on January 3, 1923, presumably of throat or lung cancer, as Mother recalls he chewed tobacco all his life and frequently coughed and spit. After enduring several more harsh winters, the family moved back to Santa Fe, where they stayed with relatives until they found a house of their own. Although the children were only teenagers, the entire family worked to support themselves. Mother worked long and hard hours six days a week at the Santa Fe Electric Laundry along with several friends and relatives.

Grandma Inés worked most days as housekeeper for the Otero and Stinson family who lived in the compound next to what is now the Matteucci Fenn Gallery near Canyon Road on the prestigious east side of Santa Fe. Miguel Otero was a well-known political figure, whose wife Katherine Stinson piloted a small plane, flying friends and visitors to nearby Indian pueblos. By 1928, my mother's family scraped together enough money to build a small adobe house on Ninita Street on the west side of Santa Fe, and the family of six moved there. Eventually most of the children married and began families of their own. Grandma Inés never remarried. She continued to work as a housekeeper, and when the older son, Genaro, returned from the Army, he

Employees of Santa Fe Electric Laundry, 1925. Senaida Ortega bottom row, seventh from left.

lived with her until her death and remained a bachelor until later in his life.

Mother and my sister Anita visited Grandma Inés regularly and took me along for the ten-block walk through fields of dirt filled with wildflowers. Grandma loved to smoke and always had her little bag of Bull Durham tobacco nearby, along with a package of thin, folded papers. She expertly rolled out a cigarette for herself and handed one to my sister, who attempted to light it while trying not to cough. Grandma Inés suffered from severe headaches most of her life, and it was not unusual to find her lying on the couch, her forehead covered with six or seven of the small blue government stamps from the Bull Durham pouch. I have yet to understand this particular remedy, but she used it often. Recently my cousin Peppy told me her physician back East had offered an explanation as to why these small papers might have been used. He surmised that when the wet papers were placed on the sides of the head, the dye from them was absorbed into the capillaries, thus relieving the headache. My grandmother died in 1949 at the age of sixty-nine.

My Father and His Family

Emilio Rodríguez Romero was born October 28, 1910, in Santa Fe at 224 Hickox Street to Albert Romero and Anastasia Rodríguez. He was the first of five children, followed by Mela, Rumaldo, Willie, and Rudy. A year or two after his birth, my grandparents moved to 1030 West Houghton Street, where they lived for the rest of their lives.

Dad grew to be six feet tall, a full ten inches taller than Mom, and a handsome man. He had straight, slicked-back black hair, brown eyes, an aquiline nose, and soft skin that was well cared for and evenly tanned from many hours spent outdoors. He was a big man with strong hands and long fingers that could be gentle, stroking a child's head softly, or firm, meting out severe punishment according to the infraction.

In his younger days, Dad wore brown suits with crisply ironed white shirts and ties with diagonal designs. His shoes were always spit-shined to a high gloss. Dad's dark hair was neatly trimmed, not a hair out of place, and he was always smooth-shaven. He liked pullover sweaters with a white shirt and tie underneath. On his right hand he wore a gold ring. He had a gentle demeanor, with a subtle sense of humor, and a full smile that immediately let you know he was friendly and you were welcome. His brown eyes sparkled with a joy for life. In his twenties, he loved to strum on an old mandolin he purchased from a musician who played in one of the bars downtown.

Although he was brought up in a strict environment, his mother doted over him, dressing him in clothes and shoes that were in fashion. As a child, he wore leather shoes, woolen socks, tweed knickers, and flannel shirts. He was provided with the latest in toys, having his own wooden rocking horse to pass the hours with. But by 1915, when my father was only five, things began to change, primarily because Grandpa Albert's salary often did not provide enough income for the family.

Every morning at six o'clock, my grandmother gave Emilio a quarter and sent him downtown. He'd buy a quarter's worth of newspapers from *The New Mexican* and walk to the La Fonda Hotel, where he sold them for most of the day. He gave the

Emilio R. Romero, 1928.

Emilio R. Romero, ca. 1913.

money he earned to his mother, who used it to buy staples—
flour, sugar, and lard. If he'd had an unusually profitable day, she
was able to buy a few pounds of beef for the next day's meal. By
the age of eight, he became a shoeshine boy, carrying his wooden
box to town each day during the summer, hanging out at the
DeVargas Hotel waiting for prospective customers to beckon.

Until the eighth grade, he attended St. Francis Parochial
School near the cathedral, where the Inn of Loretto now stands.
He then began working full-time to help support the family,
which by then included five children. In 1924, at the age of four-
teen, he was hired by Mr. Gardesky to work as a soda jerk at
Capital Pharmacy on the corner across from the La Fonda Hotel.
Even then, Grandma kept him in crisply ironed white shirts,
providing a clean one each day as he prepared for work. The
pharmacy was a popular hangout for teenagers of that era, where
they sat in wooden booths or stools at the counter and drank
fountain sodas and milkshakes. Emilio was a respectful, outgoing, and popular young man, well-liked by his employer who
paid him twelve dollars per week.

In 1928 he and Grandpa Romero worked for Old Man Sauter,
hauling wood from the Pecos Valley. Sauter and his partner provided the truck, kept one load of wood, and gave them the other,
which they sold to the coal company. Always industrious, Dad
sought work that would improve his status in life and bring a little more income to the family. In the summer of 1929 he traveled to Leadville, Colorado, and worked as a laborer, digging
trenches for $1.75 an hour and returning home every couple of
weeks to bring his paycheck. It was during this year that he met
my mother, Senaida, in Santa Fe.

Dad was the keeper of family history and legends, and as we
grew into adulthood he sat at the dinner table, chain-smoking
Salem cigarettes and drinking Budweiser beer, reminiscing
about his family and Santa Fe. It seemed that during my childhood there were no strangers in Santa Fe. Dad could walk from
one end of San Francisco Street to the other and probably greet
everyone with *"Buenos días le dé Dios"* at least fifty times.
Stopping to chat with most of these people, it could take an hour
to walk the three short blocks across downtown.

Emilio R. Romero, First
Holy Communion, 1917.

During these after-dinner conversations, he recalled details
from the past such as when a grist mill was in operation and
wheat was threshed on Don Diego Street. He said, "They had to
have a little irrigation to make an 'era,' *y una era* was about, say,
a hundred feet round, and they started putting the mud real
thick, mixing it around. *Batirlo y batirlo, y batirlo asina*, mixing it like this, two or three times until you had this much mud
solid, deep, so that it would dry evenly, *porque iban a traer
cabras*, they were going to bring in the goats. A lot of times
when you wanted to thresh the wheat, *entiendes, echaban todo
el trigo allá*, they'd put all the wheat over there, *con ti paja y
todo, y traiban las cabras y le daban vuelta y vuelta, hasta que*
the wheat was threshed." He also described how at least fifty
goats were herded into the circle of dried mud, and the goats
trampled the wheat continuously until it was threshed. The

men would then take their shovels, raise the wheat, and toss it around so the wind would clean it. Because we were accustomed to flour bought from the store down the street, we listened with great interest as he described these exotic steps, and I was glad we didn't have to participate in this tedious process.

Most of the homes in our neighborhood were occupied by aunts, uncles, cousins of varying degrees, and my father's parents, who lived a few houses down across the street from us. My grandmother Anastasia Rodríguez was born in Santa Fe in 1888 and married Albert Romero on September 27, 1909. They moved into the Romero family home on Hickox Street (now Paseo de Peralta) until their house was built on Houghton Street. She was always there for us, not only as protection, but also for an endless supply of food, especially tortillas. I liked Grandma's house—it was warm and inviting, and typical of most of the houses in the neighborhood, it was built to suit her family's needs at the time of construction. Unlike homes built today, houses then were sometimes built a room at a time, usually with a kitchen and one or two rooms to start with. There was rarely a floor plan, other than one drawn in the dirt with a stick or on a piece of butcher paper. Grandma's house was no exception, although by the time I was born, two of the bedrooms had been converted to a dining room and living room, and an indoor bathroom had been added. It wasn't a large house, but there was always room for everyone. Entering through the enclosed portal next to the kitchen, we could walk through the entire house and exit at the portal's other door, never passing through the same room twice. It even had a hallway leading from my grandparents' bedroom to the living room. In square footage, her house was larger than ours. I find it strange that I refer to it as *her* house, since my grandfather also lived there, but we all knew she was the matriarch of the family.

Like all of the houses in the neighborhood, the house was built of adobe blocks but plastered over with a gray, heavily textured plaster and painted rose pink, which distinguished it from the other houses that were mostly white. It had a double row of

Anastasia Rodríguez, First Holy
Communion, 1895, Santa Fe.

red bricks on the edge of the roof (made by the prisoners at the
penitentiary), now known as Territorial style, and a white picket
fence in front of the house, which was replaced some years later
by an adobe wall. Dad fondly recalled, "My mother's sister
Josefíta was an *enjarradora*. She would apply mud plaster to the
walls with her bare hands. My mother would help her by hand-
ing her the buckets of mud mixed with straw. One time, after
spending many hours finishing the walls of the house, a great

cloudburst of rain came and washed all their hard work away, because the mud didn't have a chance to dry."

Inside Grandma's house, the ceilings were several feet higher than those in other houses. The kitchen and bathroom walls were painted in varying shades of enamel paints bought downtown at Theo Roybal's general store. The kitchen was good-sized and laid out efficiently for the space it occupied. The woodstove stood against the center of the right wall, with a pile of wood stacked neatly next to it. A pine box with various sizes of wood slivers sat next to the wall. These were the *palitos*, small pieces of kindling that boys generally were awoken to gather every morning if they failed to keep the kindling box full. The glassed cabinet on the left side of the room held the many cups and dishes on the top side and canned goods on the bottom. A large flour bin was in the center. The cabinet was periodically repainted with white enamel paint. On the left side of the room, next to the window looking out into the small yard shaded by a huge apricot tree, sat a table with four or five chairs that were rarely vacant. If one of my grandmother's sons wasn't sitting in them, one of the grandchildren was.

The dining room was next to the kitchen, with a highly waxed wooden table and eight chairs, a sideboard, and a glassed *trastero* for Grandma's better china. I don't recall a regular meal ever being served in the dining room. Except for Thanksgiving, meals were always served in the kitchen. But this was still a special room because its furnishings reflected a social status not present in other neighborhood houses. With the exception of the Martínez house, I believe Grandma's was the only house of that age on the entire street that had what we considered a formal dining room.

Grandma never stopped cooking, since it was her passion. Most of the day, especially at mealtimes, an endless stream of children, grandchildren, and other relatives went in and out of the house. She raised my cousins Ramona and Gilbert, and later, two of Ramona's children lived with her, and she still had energy left over for the rest of us. Her favorite spot was next to the woodstove, where she soaked pieces of tortilla in pan drippings, scraping up every last drop left by the meat and potatoes

Anastasia and Alberto
Romero, 1950s.

she had just served the chosen many. This memory of her next
to the stove was one my dad would often recall years later.

She was a beautiful woman with long, dark silver-gray hair,
which she wore fashioned in a single braid or chignon bun close
to the back of her neck. Her skin was soft and light, and she had
full lips and a Spanish nose. She was pleasantly plump, always
happy, and she raised her five children with tenderness and a
firm hand. She had large, abundant arms that flopped rhythmically as she rolled out the many tortillas for dinner with a
wooden rolling pin originally cut from a broom handle. She wore
cotton dresses that buttoned up the front. She loved material
with small polka dots and wore it often. Her shoes were shiny
black leather pumps, with a small heel for everyday wear, laced
a few inches up the front, and tied in a bow well below the
ankle. Grandma's nylons weren't sheer; they were a beige cotton

material. I watched with fascination as she pulled them up to just below her knee and proceeded to wind the excess material into a knot that she tucked under the fold at the knee. With just that expertly rolled knot, her cotton nylons would stay in place for the entire day.

Grandma Anastasia took care of her mother, affectionately called Mama Vía, who was in her late nineties. Mama Vía's full name was Ciprianita Trujillo and she was born in Chimayó on September 25, 1853. She married Manuel de Jesús Rodríguez y Valencia, who was born in Santa Fe on April 16, 1849. They had a large family, including my grandmother and her sister Josefita and four boys, Narciso, Luis, Cayetano, and Pablo. Three other brothers succumbed to scarlet fever as infants. I recall my great-grandmother had hair like spun silver, which Grandma patiently braided and pinned to her head like a crown. Grandma kept her clean and spotless, always dressed in black, a color she preferred after her husband's death, with a starched and pressed white apron tied neatly around her thin waist. My sister Anita and cousin Ramona often slept in the same bed with her. In the middle of the night the girls would start giggling, and with closed eyes, Mama Vía would reach over and deliver a stinging pinch every time they moved. After a few painful pinches, the girls would finally fall asleep. Since Mama Vía lived with Grandma Romero, we rarely traveled to her home on Pacheco Street, which by that time she had sold to one of her sons for a hundred dollars. But on special occasions such as weddings and wakes, the entire family gathered there.

Grandpa Albert Romero was born in Santa Fe in 1889. He, too, was from a large family. His brothers were Elías, Manuel, Francísco, and Tony. He had only one sister, Gregorita, whom we knew as Goya, who ironed clothes for a living and remained a spinster all of her life, caring for her brothers' children. His father Tomas, my great-grandfather, was a city policeman who patrolled the bars, pool halls, and nightclubs. Grandpa's brother Francisco was a tailor who owned a dry-cleaning service and generously provided complete outfits for his many nephews' First Holy Communion services. For any occasion requiring a suit, he would have been insulted had they not asked him first.

Rumaldo Romero, my
father's brother, 1940s.

He used the finest cloth available, closely following the styles of
the era.

As children, we spent little time with Grandpa, since he
was always working, sometimes holding down two jobs to
make ends meet. In 1922 he worked as a laborer for the Denver
company contracted to pave the streets of Santa Fe with
cement. He later worked for Santa Fe Builders as a laborer six
days a week, earning $2.50 per day, unloading lumber from the
railcars that came directly to the company lot. They were paid
every Saturday at six o'clock, and Grandma waited for him at
Ballard's No. 4 Store, which stayed open until ten o'clock to

Boss with laborers on paving project, 1922, Santa Fe, in front of the New Mexican building. Albert Romero in second row, black hat.

accommodate the workers. After shopping for groceries, they would take a taxi home, which cost twenty-five cents.

Grandpa also worked as a janitor at Harrington Junior High, a few blocks from our neighborhood, but had difficulty operating the steam heat boilers and transferred instead to the smaller Kaune Elementary School. In the late 1920s, when my father negotiated a contract with the newly formed U.S. Forest Service, he shared the contract with Grandpa and several other relatives. Dad's job was erecting barbed-wire fences around all U.S. Forest property in northern New Mexico. They worked away from home five days a week and returned on weekends. During this period they fenced much of the forest surrounding the Pecos Valley. On each trip home, Dad brought several blue spruce trees that he planted on the grounds adjoining St. Francis Cathedral. On the day they were to return home for the weekend, Grandpa Albert and another worker were tightening the fence to make sure it would hold until their return on Monday. As he wound the wire tightly around the post, it snapped and hit him in the eye, knocking him to the ground. Dad carried him to the old, green Forest Service truck and drove as fast as he could down the mountain to St. Vincent's Hospital in downtown Santa Fe. The doctor brought grim news to the family that Grandpa Albert had lost his eye. Not wanting the hassle of a glass eye, he opted for a frosted lens on his glasses instead. Unfortunately, the U.S. government only paid him $275 for the injury he received, since technically he was not their employee.

Grandpa was tall and thin, with a shock of black hair with thread-like, silver-gray streaks running through it. He had an easy smile, which generously showed his crooked teeth, discolored brown from so many years of tobacco smoking. I recall he always wore khaki work pants with suspenders, a long-sleeved, checkered flannel shirt, and heavy work boots. He was a man of few words, and we all knew Grandma was the boss of that household. He loved to dance, and at every gathering he was light on his feet as he twirled each of us to the tempo of the music.

My Siblings

My parents Senaida Ortega and Emilio Romero met in 1929 and married in June of 1930, when my mother was three months pregnant and just a month shy of her twenty-first birthday. When Grandma Inés discovered Mother was pregnant, she became very angry. Unmarried pregnant women of that generation were looked upon with disdain, and Grandma would have none of it. After visiting with Dad's parents, the wedding was arranged. The impromptu wedding ceremony was held at Grandma Inés's house on Ninita Street, with members of both families in attendance. A justice of the peace officiated. The young couple went to live on Houghton Street in the tiny two-room house behind my grandparents' home.

Uncle Willie recalls that when my sister Anita was born, Grandma Inés was still angry and told my parents they couldn't baptize her since they had chosen to consummate their relationship in the shadows of the night. This would be their punishment. Grandma Romero slammed her fist on the kitchen table when she heard this and arranged for the baptism. Eventually

The first four: Bobby, Anita, Emilio, Jr., and Jimmy, 1939.

the in-laws were able to work out their differences, since the culture did not allow for dissension among family members.

My sister Anita Faustina was their firstborn. She was born two days before Christmas in 1930. Anita was the beauty of the family, with honey-brown hair and eyes and beautiful skin to match. She had perfectly arched eyebrows and a porcelain-like complexion. She loved to dress up and wear matching silk ribbons in her hair.

Emilio Estevan was born in 1932. As children we called him "Boy," which has continued throughout his life. He had neatly side-parted hair, light brown eyes, and an engaging smile. As a child he loved to draw and spent many hours doodling and sketching on any paper he could find. He was usually quiet and managed to stay out of trouble. The most serious trouble he ever got in was for painting a large swastika on the portal of the Catanachs' house across the street. We thought nothing of it until the following day when their oldest boy chased Emilio down and beat him up. Eventually he began to put his artistic talents to good use. When María's Mexican Kitchen opened on

Senaida Romero,
wedding, 1930.

Cordova Road, he carved the large wooden sign with the restaurant's name and a Mexican wearing a sombrero leaning up against a cactus. The fifty-dollar sign still sits attached to the exterior wall, although the restaurant changed hands a number of years ago and the sign has been repainted several times.

Robert, "Bobby," was the third child, born in 1934. He was born with a head of dark, wavy hair and dark eyes with a mischievous glint. When he was old enough to walk, he spent most of his waking hours outdoors, which resulted in year-round tanned skin. He was noticeably different from the rest of us, a nonconformist bent on breaking the rules. At Christmastime when Santa Claus visited the plaza, an event sponsored by the 20–30 Rifle Club, children and teens stood in line to receive small paper bags filled with hard candy, a pat on the shoulder, a Merry Christmas, and a

Bobby at Springer
Boys School, 1951.

ho-ho-ho. Bobby would stand in line and then exchange jackets
with one of his friends and get in line again. He was thoughtful,
caring, and compassionate but always in trouble. His police
record began when he was ten. The first time the police knocked
at the door with Bobby in tow, my parents thought he was tucked
safely in bed, like the rest of us. He dressed differently, stayed out
late, had problems in school. Bobby always believed he was the
black sheep of the family, and it seemed like he went out of his
way to prove it, which resulted in various stints in the juvenile
offender reform school in Springer, New Mexico, and later, the
State Penitentiary. (In later years, though, after turning his life
around, he had begun to follow the footsteps of my parents and
was creating beautiful items handcrafted out of tin.)

When Santiago Fernando, "Jimmy," was born in 1937, the
boys outnumbered the girls three to one. Jimmy also had dark
hair, but large, hazel green eyes and a chubby face. He was named
after our maternal grandfather, Santiago Ortega. Jimmy was a
friendly, good-natured child with an easygoing disposition.

Marie and Rosalie, 1944.

It seems Mother was with child every two years, and the birth of my sister Rosalia Anastasia in 1939 didn't change that. She was named Rosalia after my mother's great-aunt, and Anastasia after my dad's mother. I was never able to say "Rosalie," so she was dubbed "Deedee," a nickname that sticks to this day. She had straight, black hair and dark brown eyes. As a child she spent a lot of time with Mother, helping her clean and cook, tasks the rest of us shied away from.

When I was born in 1942, I evened out the boy-girl ratio, three to three. But everyone noted that I was different. I was a small child with very light skin and a head full of curly red hair. Right off the bat I was "Daddy's girl," not because I was special but because I was different. I generated a lot of interest with my Shirley Temple curls, particularly when the family traveled to San Diego the following year so that the adults could work in an airplane factory. Missing their own children, sailors docked in the harbor took time to hold me in their arms as my proud father looked on. (I'm still a sucker for a man in uniform!)

Mother had a six-year reprieve from her biennial task of giving birth until May of 1948, when my youngest brother, Ricardo Patricio, was born. I was six years old, and I remember a woman arriving at our house, spending a few minutes with Mother, and then shooing everyone out of the living room. I couldn't figure out what was going on. My dad and uncles carried the kitchen table into the room and the woman (who years later I discovered was a *partera*, or midwife) covered the table with several cotton sheets and blankets. I watched this scene unfold with great interest, peeking through the crack in the door.

Mother was sitting in a chair next to the makeshift bed and looked as though she was in great pain. I thought maybe she had a headache, and I started forward to see if she needed an aspirin, but the woman gave me a look that stopped me, and she gently but firmly escorted me out of the room. Since the living room door swelled in the summer and would never close completely, I repositioned myself next to it and listened and watched for any clues. I observed as Mom paced around the room, stopping every so often to catch her breath and hold on to her back and swollen stomach. I realized that she was experiencing pains that seemed to come and go. Frightened, I ran into the kitchen where Dad was playing cards with his brother, Uncle Rumaldo, and told him what was happening. He chuckled and told me to go to bed, that Mom was about to have a baby and everything would be all right. I walked back to the crack in the door thinking, *Baby! From where! Is that why that woman is here; is she bringing us a baby!*

Children never knew where babies came from. It seemed as though they just appeared magically, not only in our household but also in others. Finally, tiring of all the commotion, I dozed off, only to have Dad wake me up to tell me I had a little brother. The next morning, the lady was gone and Mom motioned me over to her bed and showed me the new baby, who looked at me with disinterest.

Pat, as we called him, was the most beautiful baby I'd ever seen. He weighed in at thirteen pounds. He was not only

Ricardo and Marie, 1950.

chubby, but also about two feet long. By the time he was two, he had become my playmate. For whatever reason, he hadn't had a haircut yet. He had long, honey-brown hair that I painstakingly curled in long ringlets. I dressed him in a turquoise-colored fiesta outfit with a long broomstick skirt and a ruffled top and took him over to Mr. Franke's house on Lomita Street to be photographed. Fortunately, my dressing him as a girl had no adverse effects in later life.

With Pat's birth, the family was complete, with an eighteen-year gap between the first and last child. By the time I was ten years old in 1952, Anita, Emilio, and Bobby had reached adulthood and moved out of the family home.

Chapter Two

THE FAMILY HOME

Dad began construction of our house on West Houghton Street in 1930, shaped from thousands of adobes that he and Grandpa Albert and two of his brothers, Rudy and Willie, made from mud mixed with straw. These were large adobe bricks made in wooden forms. I imagine the piles of adobes in the vacant lot must have resembled stacks of giant brown dominoes waiting to be played. Uncle Frank Rivera helped to dig the foundation, which was filled with cement mixed in a wheelbarrow. The adobes were then stacked one on top of the other with a thick layer of mud in between. The walls were almost a foot thick, and when completed, the house had three rooms, the largest of which had a fireplace. The smallest had a woodstove for cooking and heating. The floors were hardwood, which Mother cleaned and oiled to a high sheen periodically. In the late 1940s, the combination kitchen/bedroom was modest but comfortable.

The woodstove in one corner served a dual purpose—cooking and warmth. My sometimes unwilling brothers kept the woodpile near the door stocked. If there was no wood, they would be awoken at five o'clock in the morning and told to go outside (even in below-zero temperatures) and gather wood for the day's fire.

In another corner was a wringer washing machine, which was filled by heating water in buckets and pouring it into the machine. Water had to be changed manually. After rinsing, the clothes were repeatedly run through the hand-cranked rollers until all the water was removed. They were hung to dry with wooden clothespins on the wire clotheslines outside: dish towels and bath towels together on the outer lines, underwear and sometimes tattered clothing on the center wire, obscured from view. When you're poor, that is one method for keeping it hidden, if only from yourself.

Furnishings in the house were simple. The walls were bare, except for a multipage wall calendar from St. Francis Cathedral, the shoemaker, or Sanco Ford Company, which hung on a nail on the kitchen wall. One or two paper prints of saints hung in simple, glassed wooden frames, and the niches in the wall above the stove and in the living room housed plaster statues depicting the Sacred Heart of Jesus or Our Lady of Fatima. On the wall next to the kitchen door, a piece of two-by-four wood, into which several large nails had been hammered, served as a makeshift coatrack. The wooden kitchen table was sturdy and had a long bench on each side, flanked by two wooden chairs. (In the 1950s, this would be replaced by a stainless steel table with a bright yellow Formica top, a style now in great demand by interior decorators.) The heavy quilts on the beds were all homemade by Mother, who saved scraps cut from discarded clothing to make the cover tops. These quilts were topped by well-worn pink or beige chenille bedspreads given to her by her older sister Sally. Some of us slept on mattresses laid on the floor in the middle room, which were then stacked on the double bed in the corner during the day, and the younger ones slept in the larger bedroom with our parents. A small bed was tucked in a corner in the kitchen, available to whomever got there first, usually one of the boys.

My parents' bedroom had a small fireplace with a brick-edged mantel, which kept the room warm, but as the winds outside changed, it sent billows of smoke into the room at unpredictable intervals. When there wasn't a fire, cold wind gusted into the room, since the chimney was built without a flue to keep the cold air out. The wooden vigas, large beams stretching across the ceiling in each room, were cleaned and oiled periodically, much like the floor. Every spring as the snow on the roof thawed and in summer when the rains came, the corners of the house leaked, necessitating rearrangement of the furniture until the roof could be patched.

A large, enclosed porch was attached to the front of the house, also built from adobes. It also had wooden beams that jutted on the outside. From our perch on its wall, we could observe life as it occurred in the neighborhood. In the summertime, an old canvas cot sat in one corner of the porch, and I recall spending many hours relaxing there in the coolness of the evening. Outside in the front yard, the apricot tree had grown so high it rested its top branches on the roof. I could climb to the higher branches and see the rooftops of the entire neighborhood. In the early years of my childhood, the front yard consisted of mostly dirt, which reached out to touch the dirt road that ran between the rows of houses. Only an occasional set of tire tracks reminded us that there was a street separating our yards.

By the mid-1950s, the outline of the street became more prominent as automobiles were more accessible through banks and finance companies. Then it seemed like three- or four-foot plastered adobe walls sprang up overnight to delineate the edges of yards and mark arbitrary property lines. We now had a new vantage point from which to watch neighborhood goings-on, or barriers to protect us from occasional barrages of rocks or snowballs. During the summertime, fruit trees bordering the house flowered with fragrant pink and white petals and later bore crops of succulent green apples and deep orange apricots. Multipurpled lilac bushes gave forth not only abundant flowers, but their pungent perfume permeated the air as well. Huge, multipetalled red and yellow chrysanthemums and zinnias filled all the spaces in between, with lavender-hued irises peeking out over the wall.

There was never a patch of grass in our yard, probably because lawn mowers were an expensive luxury, as was the grass seed. The shade provided from the trees kept the ground cool, and lying

Marie with chickens in the yard, 1944.

in the middle of the yard on the soft moist soil was just as comfortable as being on a patch of green grass, or so I imagined.

In the early days, we shared an outhouse in the yard next
door with relatives living nearby. It was often a fearful place for
a child. For whatever reason, these wooden structures were a little rickety, and on cold days the wind whipped right through the
cracks, freezing skin in places we didn't even know could freeze.
I worried about falling into the unknown depths, never to be
seen again, as I imagined the hole in the ground to be hundreds
of feet deep. Not only that, but I always figured that bugs and
spiders of every deadly variety were lined up on the walls, ceiling, and under the stool, waiting to bite our behinds. To top it
off, Mom had all kinds of horror stories about pregnant women
having lost their unborn babies in these abysses. I imagine the
stories might not have been true, but they sure made us do our
business quickly. That is, unless some jokester decided to wedge
a few obstacles against the door so it wouldn't open, eventually
letting you out after much screaming and begging. Nonetheless,
nobody ever tarried in the outhouse, particularly as the sun

started to set. (If the need arose at night, there was a large tin can for that purpose; otherwise you had to hold your business until morning.)

I couldn't understand why there were two seats available in the outhouse. I thought this was a private function, not a community one. Long before Charmin was introduced to bathrooms across America, the only available tissue paper in these outdoor bathrooms were the Sears and "Monkey" Wards catalogs. When a new and much larger kitchen and an indoor bathroom were added to our house in the 1950s, our lives changed considerably. This small eight-by-twelve foot room provided us with a luxury we'd never experienced—privacy. Eventually, with the advent of more indoor bathrooms in the neighborhood, the old outdoor privy was abandoned. Not much later, it was demolished and the remaining hole filled with rocks and dirt. A large apricot tree grew near the spot, but we were never too anxious to eat its spindly fruit, believing it had grown with the wrong kind of fertilizer.

We usually bathed weekly on Saturday nights by heating many gallons of water in a large kettle on top of the woodstove. One of us sat in the *cajete*, a large tin tub, and we were soaped down and then rinsed with warm water from another pot. When the water reached room temperature, it was emptied from the tub and replaced with more hot water. As one child was dried off, the other jumped in for his or her bath. Lucky was the one who got into the tub first, usually the youngest. After one or two baths, particularly if the boys went first, the water was ready to be thrown out. Dad would drag the heavy tub out the kitchen door and empty it by the trees near the wall, being careful in winter not to let it run toward the house; otherwise it formed a large ice puddle by morning. On freezing nights it was too cold to bathe, and we opted for just wiping off our skin with a washcloth. But the boys were usually fairly grungy, even in the wintertime.

It was such a relief when indoor plumbing was installed in the early 1950s. It allowed us to have a warm bath, whether we needed one or not. The new bathroom was warm and inviting, half the size of a small bedroom. The enamel walls were painted bright canary yellow and one could escape to the luxury of a bubble bath on days when siblings were interested in other activities. With any spare change we could find, Rosalie and I purchased inexpensive perfumed bath crystals and bubbling oils at the five-and-dime. Once in a while we could experience this lavish comfort without someone banging on the door and hollering that they needed to use the bathroom. More often than not, bathing still had to be accomplished quickly, since there were five children and two adults living in the household.

Unlike some of today's tract neighborhoods, not all houses were of equal size. For instance, the Martínezes were not only our good neighbors, but also cousins on my dad's maternal side. Their house was warm and cozy and looked like a mansion compared to ours in my eyes. It, too, was of adobe, but it had style, with white-plastered exterior walls, a well-groomed yard, a garage, and even a dog house. When we wanted to play with any of our ten cousins, we knocked on the kitchen screen door and waited for one of them to come out. We were rarely invited in because Mrs. Martínez was usually cooking one of the three meals that were attended by their entire family. I was fascinated by the size of their kitchen table. It was solid wood and probably twelve feet long to accommodate the whole family at one sitting. It had long wooden benches on each side and chairs at the head and foot of the table for the parents. The inside of the house was huge in our eyes, and they didn't need to stack the children one on top of the other. It never ceased to amaze me how such a large family could coexist with each other. They were like stair steps, each child just a little older and taller than the previous one. In addition, the grandparents, Tío Fortino and his wife Josefita, lived next to them in a small adobe house and they were included for most meals.

Across from the Martínez house, the Tapia family lived in a large L-shaped compound with a few adobe rooms and many chicken coops. They, too, were a large family who raised chickens and goats. The children all had sandy brown hair and greenish eyes and were close in age to us. To the left of their house lived the Apodaca family, another large family with children ranging in age much like our own. The Gonzales clan lived next to them on the right, in a small house accommodating yet another large family. Next to our house lived my Uncle Joe and his wife Mela, who was my dad's only sister. Their two children were Ramona and Gilbert. Next to them and across from Grandma's house were Uncle Rumaldo and Aunt Lena, another one of my dad's brothers. They had five children, all fairly close in age: Teresa, Orlando, Christella, Gene, and Lillian.

Other relatives, my dad's first and second cousins, lived around the bend and included the Corderos, Romeros, and Gutiérrezes, with only two or three children. Although we were related, we didn't spend as much time with these families as we did with our closer relatives and neighbors, but we happily assembled at weddings, baptisms, and other neighborhood events.

Chapter Three

EARLY CHILDHOOD DAYS

In 1955 the population of Santa Fe was thirty thousand, and although it was larger than we imagined it to be, we were limited mostly to our area of town and neighborhood. Until recently I was unaware that in 1950 there were seventy-five grocery stores, twenty-four gas stations, fifteen beauty shops, and eleven barbershops, along with about forty lawyers and eight taxicabs. These numbers would almost double by 1956.

We grew up semi-poor but happy in an era of massive changes rocking the country, changes that filtered down slowly into New Mexico. The Southwest experienced Depressions long after the rest of the country had begun to regain financial stability. Rock and roll music landed in our living rooms through the local AM radio station but didn't create the same frenzy it did in the major cities around the country. As a child, I assumed my family and most of the neighborhood were outwardly unaffected by politics and the world in general. Most of the national news came to us through the radio or newsreels at the movies, but our daily focus was on more pressing issues, primarily home and school. Sputnik encircled the earth in 1957, yet that event had little impact on our lives, not because we lacked interest, but because nobody in our family was sophisticated enough to understand satellites and space travel. Far more important were events happening in our homes, not in the world. We did not discuss world events at the dinner table.

In the late 1920s telephone lines popped up in Santa Fe, with six- or eight-party lines being the norm. There were always business phones, but few residential, at least in our neighborhood. My grandparents, the Martínez family, and the Catanach family installed phone service in the 1940s, but we waited until the 1950s when Ma Bell was spreading her wires into the recesses of the city. The lines were two- or four-party. Our phone number was Yucca 3–3691, and we generally shared the line with neighbors, although occasionally there would be a voice on the phone we didn't recognize. Residents visited over the wires by the hour, carrying on as though they were in the same room, some hogging the line on a first come, first serve basis, while irate parties slammed down the phone noisily if they couldn't place their calls. There was no such thing as a private conversation—everyone knew everyone else's business. The telephone company had unwittingly created a way for citizens bored with their lives to listen in on other people's *mitote*, the local gossip.

Naturally, many of my early childhood memories have to do with school days. My older siblings' Catholic education began at St. Francis Parochial School, located in downtown Santa Fe next to the La Fonda Hotel, where the hotel's parking garage is today. By the time I was of school age, a newer school had been built on upper Alameda Street. I attended the first two grades under the ear-pinching discipline of Sister Josina, a barely five foot ball of boundless energy and terror. She taught first grade there and also taught my father in 1916, thirty years earlier at the old *parroquia* school. My sister Rosalie recalls, without fondness, that Sister Josina carried a stick with her at all times. "For any infraction, no matter how minor, she would make us hold our hands out. She would whack them severely. We were punished for talking, poor handwriting, incomplete lessons, and any number of reasons. Not much taller than most of the students, she was mean and intimidating." My cousin Teresa recalls having a Mickey Mouse watch that she lovingly wore. One day she allowed her little brother Orlando to wear it to school, after admonishing him to not dare lose it or he'd have hell to pay. Orlando must have had a bad day with Sister Josina, because she insisted he give the watch to her as punishment for whatever violation he had committed. Much to Teresa's dismay, she was never able to retrieve the coveted watch from the nun. Although we didn't find Sister Josina to be warm and loving as we imagined nuns should be, many of her former students recalled her with great fondness. She lived well into her nineties.

Occasionally there were humorous moments on the playground. Sister Mark Marie often had playground duty and participated in child play with delight. One day a big gust of wind came blowing through the playground, and we held on to our skirts to keep them from being lifted up to expose our underwear. Sister's black veil with white surplice attached was suddenly blown from her head and we chased it toward the fence to retrieve it. As the wind died down, the students stared in shock at the sight of Sister's shaved head. In one motion she grabbed her veil, placed it firmly around her head, and declared recess to be over as she ran into the building to compose herself.

After second grade, I attended Santa Fe public schools. Whether out of boredom or curiosity, I counted my footsteps each day as I walked to elementary school, about five blocks from home. This went on for years, my goal being to cut a few steps off each trip, or at least equal the steps from the day before. There were more than five thousand steps leading to elementary and junior high, located at the bottom of a hill and facing each other on East Booth Street. I estimate that I walked more than two and a half million steps a year for nine years before high school, located a block north of the plaza downtown. High school meant three more freezing winters, walking twice as far. (Actually, I skipped third grade, so deduct two million steps for that year, but add another two and a half million for coming home for lunch most days.)

Sometimes on the way home from school, I stopped to pick or smell the flowers, depending on whether someone was watching. As I walked past the Salmon Greer Mansion on Don Gaspar Avenue, I was in awe of its majesty, the riches it reflected. It was the biggest and most luxurious house around, with a two-story pitched roof building, a nonexistent feature in our neighborhood, and a welcoming porch along the front. I thought that it resembled a big plantation house, like the one in *Gone with the Wind*. The soft grass surrounding the house was green and plush and more inviting than anywhere else in town. The trees were taller, and the fruit was ripe and juicy. (My brothers weren't interested in the house itself; they were interested only in the cherries, apples, and plums, which, without invitation, they harvested each season after dark.) The circular driveway housed a shiny new Cadillac, which kept company with several other luxury cars. All these details added up to a world all its own in a neighborhood among large, gracious homes, of which this was the most elegant. From the sidewalk, I peered through the circular wrought-iron sections of the wall and imagined what splendors lay inside, what delicacies were eaten at their meals, servants adding unimagined ease and luxury—a royal existence we would never experience. I imagined the family had few worries and that they ate their meals on silver plates using golden spoons. As I walked away with my handful of pilfered marigolds and zinnias, I thought to myself, "And I'll bet they never eat tortillas, either."

When I was eight, I received a musical gift, but not the piano I dreamed of. Dad brought home an accordion and decided I was going to learn to play it. It was a Hohner brand, with two rows of buttons on the right and base buttons on the left. The wood surface was intricately decorated with scrolls and flowers and covered with many coats of varnish to make it shine. It was a rectangular wooden box that loudly exhaled air when a button was pressed.

At first, I looked at this instrument with great disdain. After all, it was not a piano. However, to show some appreciation, I dutifully fiddled with it, listening for sounds that might resemble music. As I sat on the porch one afternoon and squeaked out

Salmon-Greer Mansion, Don Gaspar Avenue, Santa Fe.

an almost recognizable rendition of "Lady of Spain," I began to enjoy my meager musical beginnings. The accordion was more versatile than a piano would have been, I mused, although I was only able to master the buttons on the right side, having no idea how to use the base buttons on the left. Since I couldn't read music, I played by ear, repeating a melody until recognition set in and I could almost play it without effort. No matter, by age ten I was playing with a group of seasoned musicians comprised of Uncle Willie on guitar, Perfidio Padilla on violin, and Eleuterio Nava on a big bass fiddle. We provided the music for every wedding, baptism, First Holy Communion, and basic get-togethers in our neighborhood and others, come rain or shine. By the time I was a teenager, these musical engagements had taken over my life.

I suspect Dad was a frustrated musician who lived vicari-ously through my weekend appearances at these functions, whether I agreed to them or not. I could pout and throw tantrums, but in the end I still had to participate. I surmised the others were far better musicians than I would ever be, and not only that, they were seasoned and older and could have probably survived quite well without my involvement. The number of tunes to be learned was mind-boggling, from "La Varsioviana" for the oldsters, to severely altered rock and roll music for the younger set, "Corrina, Corrina" and "You Ain't Nothin' But a Hound Dog." Dad's particular favorite was "Little Brown Jug," and we played it for him at every opportunity. I didn't know the key of A from the key of D, but the other musicians did. Every time we played, it took me a while to get the tempo, but eventually I jumped in. The group played right over me when I missed a key and continued on when my hands tired or I didn't know the melody.

Whenever there was a wedding, we knew we would have a good time. Sometimes the dance would last for hours after dark, and most of the children fell asleep under the tables. During the last dance, everyone pinned money to the bride's veil or the groom's jacket, paying for a dance with him or her. By this time many of the guests might be a bit tipsy, tripping over each other or us while they danced. But all in all, we played with gusto, and when my small hands grew tired, the band still played on. My uncle usually slipped me a ten-dollar bill at the end of the music, which was the highlight of my day.

In the fourth grade, my parents scraped up the money for me to take music lessons, because I believed the violin was more sophisticated than the lowly accordion. It wasn't too long before the music teacher, Ms. Emily DuBold, realized I would never be a concert violinist and as a humanitarian gesture suggested to my parents that my lessons be discontinued. Besides, I suspect the twice weekly lessons and the violin rental were more expensive than a month's groceries. The required melodies were foreign to me, hardly the toe-tapping *rancheras* our group played. The music of New Mexico was in my veins, and violin lessons did not enhance my talent.

Chapter Four

FOOD AND MEALTIMES

We all had assigned places at the kitchen table by an unwritten law, which held that if you sat in a spot often enough, it was yours. The old wooden table had been replaced by two stainless-steel, tubular-legged tables (now called Art Deco) with yellow Formica tops covered with a long red-and-white–checkered plastic oilcloth purchased at the five-and-dime. Mother sat at the head of the table, presumably so she would be closer to the stove, making it easier to reach everything Dad requested: *la sal*, *la pimienta*, *el trapo* (cloth napkin), *una tortilla*, another fork, *otra cerveza*, and so on. He sat to her right and was waited on like royalty, never lifting a finger except to eat. If anything was out of his reach, she quickly retrieved it for him. Dinner was generally a quiet affair, depending on Dad's mood. He usually consumed several beers after work and was subject to unpredictable mood changes. The hour was for eating and few relevant discussions took place. Dad read the newspaper as he ate, leisurely finishing off a last beer before retiring for the night. My sister Rosalie and I had the task of cleaning up, making sure all the dishes, pots, and pans were washed and ready for the next day's use, although she recalls I often had a number of excuses for why I couldn't help with the dishes that night.

We always had enough food to go around, as the staples were beans, flour tortillas, chile, posole, and a *caldito* (soup) made from chopped beef, potatoes, onions, and flour. Mother boiled pitchers of salted milk to be poured into bowls of atole, a soupy blue corn gruel. She also made pans of hot red chile, spoonfuls of which she added to the c*haquehue*, a thick and chunky meal also made from blue corn, but with a grittier texture than atole has. She often served macaroni with a tomatoey sauce. We made cheese at home from boiled whole milk, to which we added storebought rennet tablets. After the cooling milk thickened, Mother wrapped it in cheesecloth to drain the remaining liquid. We ate thin slices of cheese with small trails of molasses dripped over it. I still search for this cheese at health food stores, hoping to once again savor the grainy, lightly salted taste. But it's never the same. In those days we used milk delivered straight from the dairy, skimming off the layer of thick cream at the top to make the cheese.

In order to keep perishable food cold, many people relied on their windowsills, where they placed meat for the next day's meal. We had an old icebox in the corner that chilled meat after the slaughter, and eggs, milk, and butter. Ice was a wintertime commodity. With early morning temperatures well below zero, Grandpa Romero cut ice from a swimming pool on Sierra Vista Court a few blocks from home and sold it to the ice company. To make ice, he and a helper filled the pool with about four inches of water. By the next morning, the water was frozen. Grandpa tied gunnysacks over his shoes to keep from slipping and then cut the ice into blocks, loading them onto his wagon and hauling them to the ice company. He would bring home any remaining blocks of ice. Ice was used only to preserve food. It was much later that we made ice for cold drinks by placing water in small aluminum trays in the freezer section of an elec-tric refrigerator.

Mother made tortillas every day. The process was easily learned, but difficult to master. Tortillas were made lovingly, always just enough for a meal. My mother's recipe was basically a few handfuls of flour, some baking powder, a sprinkle of salt, and three fingers full of lard, with enough warm water to mix it together. As she added the salt, she would make the sign of the cross with it to bless the dough. She would knead the dough to form a large ball, and then methodically pluck small handfuls of dough and roll them into ping-pong–sized balls. With the *bolillo*, a rolling pin made from a piece of broomstick, she rolled the dough balls out on a lightly floured wooden cutting board. The rolling out of the dough had a rhythm to it in order to make a perfect circle. The bolillo rolled over the dough ball a few times, and then Mother turned the dough a little and rolled again until the tortilla was the size and shape she wanted, about seven inches around and a quarter inch or less thick. During this process, her thin gold wedding band made a clacking sound against the rolling pin. *Clackety clack clack clack. Clackety clack clack clack.*

Each tortilla was baked on the comal, a flat, round piece of metal placed over the fire on the stove, until the dough was bubbly and evenly covered with brown and black singe marks, and then grasped quickly with deft fingers and turned to cook on the other side. Within moments the heady aroma of this toasted flatbread would fill the kitchen. When cooked, the tortillas were placed in a thick cotton tea towel, el trapo, where they nestled in their warmth like stacks of pancakes. When the last tortilla hit the grill, it was only moments until dinner would be served. At mealtime, we used triangular pieces of tortilla torn by hand to scoop juicy brown pinto beans generously mixed with green chile and meat. By this means, the tortilla retained much of the bean juice without becoming soggy. Other times we smoothed creamy butter on the hot tortilla, and it oozed out of the corners of our mouths as we tried to keep the butter from melting too quickly. It was easy to devour many of these flavorful flatbreads at one sitting.

Crops of green chile were abundant during mid-September each year, and Mother roasted many bagsful outside on a metal grill placed over a smoldering fire. She turned the long green chile peppers frequently to keep them from burning. She accomplished this by quickly grasping the hot stem and rotating the chile so it cooked on both sides. Rosalie and I helped peel the fire-hot chiles, which Mother tied together with a string and wove like a garland through the clothesline to dry, covering them with cheesecloth to keep the flies away. Once dry, the chile was stored in a pillowcase for winter meals. If a freezer was available, we placed the peeled chile in plastic bags and froze it. Uncle Rudy loved to eat green chile, the hotter the better. When a mere spoonful would burn our tongues and singe our lips, he heaped a more than generous serving on a tortilla and proceeded to eat as though there was no fire to it. Dad chuckled as he surmised Rudy must have burned off his taste buds a long time ago, because the average person couldn't have eaten one-tenth of the chile wrapped in that tortilla.

Unharvested green chile left on the vine turned red and dried. This was later gathered and tied into *ristras*, long strings of various hues of red chile that hung to dry on nails in portals all around Santa Fe. A meal that included red chile served not only to clear one's sinus passages, but also made eyes water and ears pop.

We always had at least a dozen chickens and a few roosters in coops or sometimes scattered in the backyard, as did most of our neighbors. It seemed each chicken knew which backyard it belonged in and never failed to respond to the beckoning call of *pew, pew, pew* heard throughout the neighborhood at feeding time. At least once a week Mom's job was to catch the chicken selected for dinner. She would grab the unfortunate chicken by the feet and twirl it overhead until it was dizzy, and then grab the newly sharpened ax and lop its head off on the chopping stump in one swift move, a process I preferred to avoid. This was a necessary skill for the women in our community, since it would be too late to start dinner if they waited until the men came home. The children's job was to soak the chicken in steamy hot water until the feathers could be easily plucked off. The stench of the wet feathers was pretty unbearable. We threatened to pinch our nostrils closed with clothespins, but the distasteful chore had to be performed often, no matter the smell or our squeamishness. Once in a while my brother Jimmy's friends, Chapo Gonzales and Ludger Lucero, were invited to dinner and

Grandma Anastasia
Romero with Gilbert
Fresquez, 1945.

immediately nominated for the onerous chicken chores. They
didn't seem to mind it as much as we did, because they
approached it as chicken warfare. But with their hefty appetites,
there were few leftovers for the next day's meal.

Mother was an old-fashioned cook but was occasionally
willing to try new versions of oldfangled inventions she saw in
the kitchens of relatives and neighbors. In the late 1940s and
early 1950s, the Presto Company made strides in improving
their line of pressure cookers, designed to cut cooking times in
half without sacrificing flavor. A pot of beans could easily be
cooked in forty-five minutes rather than all day, and a pot roast
could be tenderized in less than half an hour. The trick was to
follow the directions to the letter; otherwise the food would
turn to mush. The heavy pan had a lid with a rubber seal that
served to retain pressure formed inside, thus allowing the food
to cook quickly. As soon as the liquid inside began to boil, a bit
of steam escaped from a hole in the lid. Then the pressure regu-
lator (or "dancer," as we called it) was placed over the hole,
simultaneously lowering the heat to the point when the dancer

moved rhythmically on top of the lid. On one occasion, Mother was preparing dinner, noticing the hands of the clock were moving quickly toward the time Dad would arrive. She checked the roast in the oven and lowered the temperature to keep it warm, and then moved the pressure cooker into the sink to run a little cold water over the pan to cool it. Without thinking, she opened the cooker without removing the dancer and we heard a loud explosion in the kitchen. We ran to her side, and there were mashed potatoes all over the ceiling and windows. Fortunately Mother escaped any serious injury, as the force of the explosion sent the potatoes flying upward, the lid still held tightly in her hand.

Christmastime additions to our menus were cinnamony pumpkin, meat, or fruit turnovers, *empanaditas*; biscochitos, anise-flavored, melt-in-your-mouth sugar cookies; and hand-wrapped tamales. The tamale process was long and time-consuming but well worth the effort. Rosalie and I sat on a tree stump in the backyard holding a cob of dried corn in each hand, grinding the cobs together until the kernels loosened and fell into the pan. The dekerneled corncobs were abrasive on small hands, and the pain in our fingers sometimes lasted several days. After rinsing the kernels, we mixed a portion of lye with water and added it to the corn, which was boiled in large vats on the stove to remove the skin. When cooled, we rinsed it over and over until no trace of skin or lye remained. We then placed the corn by the handful into the hand-cranked grinder and ground it until coarse. We alternated this chore since it, too, contributed to sore arm muscles. We then made the masa mixture by adding lard and meat broth and kneaded it to the consistency of thick oat-meal. The dried corn husks were soaked until soft, wiped dry, and then separated into layers to house the tamale mixture; then a red chile with meat center was added. Finally, with the husk folded over, the edges were neatly tied with long strips of the husks. For mealtime, we steamed the tamales in a large pot on the stove, and the aroma permeated the air, traveling with a breeze from room to room and outside into the yard where we counted the hours until dinnertime. I preferred my tamales without chile, and Mother dutifully made special batches for me that resembled fat hot dogs, trimming the edges to a point and making sure two or three were included in the pot.

Bread pudding, or *sopa*, was also added to the holiday table. It was made from layers of toasted or dried bread and covered with small slices of longhorn cheddar and raisins, over which a syrupy mixture was poured before it was baked in the oven. (Some years later I discovered this dessert was actually called *capirotada*, but to us it was s*opa*.)

Rosalie's job was to bake bread almost every Saturday. The yeasty aroma of fresh-baked bread saturated the air and drifted out into the neighborhood, and by Sunday dinner, none remained. We devoured it with gobs of butter from the creamery, sometimes eating more bread than the food it accompanied. Mom baked Parker House rolls, which could give any local bakery stiff competition. At Easter-time she baked hot cross buns, which had an abundance of cardamom seeds to give them a spicy flavor.

One thing I remember fondly is being introduced the fine art of coffee drinking. Grandma Romero would pour a small cup of strong coffee from a polka-dot blue metal pot she kept on the stove. She recycled the coffee grounds several times a day by adding fresh coffee to the original early morning grounds. Feeling very important, I would pour several ounces of cream into my cup and add as many spoonfuls of sugar I could get away with, not realizing both the canned coffee and those precious white crystals were a valuable commodity in neighborhood kitchens.

Our neighborhood was made up of about eighteen families, mostly poor or middle-class blue collar workers. In our world, the differences between white-collar and blue-collar workers were vast, because white-collar workers received their paychecks regularly and never seemed to worry about strikes. Although Dad worked steadily over the years for the Forest Service and then the Zia Company in Los Alamos, there were periods of layoffs or labor strikes. The strikes lasted as little as a week and as long as three months. As a young girl, I didn't understand what a strike was, but I understood that people stopped working periodically. I spent a lot of time worrying about where our food would come from, as I overheard Mother confide in Aunt Sally that we had no money since Dad wasn't working. During lean times families took care of each other. Uncle Rudy periodically brought bags of groceries filled with everything necessary for our large family to survive. In addition, Mother was an industrious canner and we always had a supply of jelly, apricots, pears, cherries, and dried apples, which saw us through long winters and the periods of unemployment. With so many relatives living nearby, I'm sure we could always borrow an egg or a cup of sugar here and there. In spite of my worrying, we never experienced true hunger—food was always on the table, and we were grateful.

Chapter Five

SHRINES, NUNS, AND SAINTS

Our home always had a shrine that sat against a corner wall in the living room, *el cuarto de recibo*, where we recited the rosary each day. The small table was covered with heavily starched mantel cloths, hand embroidered and with crocheted edges. Back then, votive candles lit at the shrines in each home in our neighborhood gave a reassuring glow on dark nights before there were street lights. Plaster of Paris statues of Jesus and Mary stood on a small table next to randomly placed rosaries and Mother's novena pamphlets. In winter, only plastic or handmade Kleenex flowers were available, which we made using bobby pins to hold the centers together, attaching long pieces of wire to create the stems. Family shrines were places where parents offered their tired souls in exchange for small favors and children prayed for fantasies, new dolls or puppies that never materialized. But we were assured the saints watched over us each day; like guardian angels they protected us as we ventured out into the unknown.

The blue-robed plaster of Paris statue of Our Lady of Fatima held center stage on the shrine, with small votive candles in colorful glass holders lit at her feet. In 1948 I earned this coveted prize for attending Mass every day in May when I was in first grade at St. Francis Parochial School. Unfortunately, the Sister didn't believe me when I handed in my carefully penciled list outlining my daily Mass attendance, signed by my parents to attest to this fact. Within hearing range of my classmates, she insisted I had not attended Mass on the last day of the month, even though my father accompanied me and we sat a few seats behind the other children. She was so insistent that she almost had me convinced she was right. Later that day, I tearfully told my father about her claim and he said to not worry because some nuns were very mean-spirited and overzealous. He never forgot the many times his knuckles were whacked with a wooden ruler by Sister Josina for the most insignificant of infractions. I couldn't believe that one of God's helpers could be so cruel to a child, and I didn't understand her insistence. It pained me to face her as the school year wound down. I remember trying to make myself small and invisible and avoided her until the last day of school. In the end, she grudgingly gave me the coveted statue, although I knew her heart wasn't in it. But I didn't care; I carried the statue home proudly and watched as Mom made her a permanent fixture on our shrine.

For as many years as I can recall, every evening after we were snuggled under the covers, Mom prayed her novenas, nine-day prayers (probably for each of us and the entire world), kneeling before the shrine. She began her prayers by reciting a rosary, which took about twenty minutes. From my room, I could hear her quiet whisper, *"Dios te salve, María..."* and *"Padre Nuestro, que estás en el cielo, santificado sea tu nombre...,"* repeated as her fingers found their way around the wooden beads, which clicked softly as the rosary swayed gently against the edge of the small table. The rhythm of her voice lulled me into a peaceful slumber. As she recited prayers from her novenas, her eyes always looked toward heaven, imploring God to grant her request. Dad often said that Mom's prayers were powerful and the Saints always listened to her. After I left home, this was one of the things I missed most. (After her death, I made it a point to pray the rosary often, knowing she would be listening. Her rosary and novena books now occupy a special place on my own shrine.)

Our family was steeped in tradition—tradition that combined not only the Catholic religion, but also our New Mexican heritage and culture as well. For females, this served as a double whammy. In our extended family, tradition dictated that young women would grow up to marry, take care of their husbands, and bear as many children as possible. Anglo girls were raised to pursue higher education, eventually marry, and bear only as many children as they wanted. In the first and second grades at St. Francis Parochial School, we were taught that inside our bodies we housed a small white heart, and every time we committed a sin, a tiny black spot appeared. Of course, if a big sin was committed, such as lying, stealing, or sassing our parents, a larger black spot would appear. This would progress until our heart would be covered with so many spots that it would turn completely black. So naturally we worked hard to avoid accumulating black spots, mostly by obeying our elders and trying to keep bad thoughts at bay. A few years ago I saw the movie *Ghost*, in which a murder victim's spirit continued to wander around on earth. In one scene a person of questionable character is killed, and some eerie spirits from beneath the surface come to retrieve him. This scene conjured up images of what we were taught as children: that if you died in a state of sin, it wouldn't be angels that would come for you.

We were not raised as Bible-reading, God-fearing children with a hell fire-and-brimstone preacher standing on a pulpit and hollering about virtue and damnation. In the Catholic Church, most priests were fairly low-key. But we were brought up believing in God, attending Mass each Sunday, being a part of such Catholic rituals as praying the rosary every day in May in honor of the Blessed Virgin Mary, and participating in Lenten and Christmas activities—not just giving lip service, but being actual players in the reenactment of church rituals. We were taught to respect our parents, our homes, and our culture. Our grandparents made sure we didn't disrespect our parents by a quiet admonition followed by a strategic arm pinch. Once in a while, when a child was being particularly ornery, my grand-mother would say in Spanish, "Well, you know what happens to bad children." We didn't know, but we could imagine.

As native New Mexicans, we lived the culture, ate the food, listened to the music, and were surrounded by traditions that rarely differed from those of our classmates. My family was bilingual but not bicultural; we were Spanish to the core. As children we never left the house without being blessed by our parents, an especially significant ritual in our household. Before venturing out of the neighborhood, we knelt before them and they placed their hands on our heads and blessed us, saying, "*En el nombre del padre, el hijo, y el espiritu santo. Que Dios bendiga a estos muchitos*" (In the name of the Father, and of the Son, and of the Holy Spirit. May God Bless these children). It wasn't until we were teenagers that this endearment outwardly embarrassed us. But no matter, blessings were always available on short notice. Grandma Romero gave her own tongue-in-cheek blessing. After she said "*Que Dios dé un Santo*" (that God give a saint), under her breath she would add, "*Pero no uno de palo*" (but not one made of wood). To her, it seemed, a wooden saint would have been the equivalent of a useless stick of wood.

Our parish church, and that of a majority of the Catholics in Santa Fe, was St. Francis Cathedral. Remodeling of this centuries-old church had begun in the 1850s by the first Archbishop of Santa Fe, the Frenchman Jean Baptiste Lamy, and it was unlike any other church in the area. Originally its thick walls had been constructed of adobe and mud, much like our homes, but the adobe walls were removed when the outer stone shell was completed in 1884. This parish church of ours was different from the other churches in Santa Fe, not only architecturally and in size, but in splendor. The interior had high vaulted ceilings and large round pillars, part of which were painted and edged in gold leaf. A green floral stencil traversed and decorated the walls the length of the church. A big-ger than life-size crucifix was strategically placed on the pillar at the left front of the altar next to the Communion rail, and since so many devout parishioners touched the nails on his feet, the paint had completely worn off. On the walls hung huge oil paintings depicting various stages in the life of Christ, and large statues

stood on pedestals around the church and seemed to watch us as
we tried to sit quietly. The stained glass windows, with images of
apostles and saints, reflected every color imaginable. The huge circular rose window above the entrance doors occupied much of my
attention when sermons started to drag. Sitting in the first few
rows of pews on the left side of the church, we were covered in a
warm glow as rainbows of color reflected off the walls as the rays
of the morning sun shone through the upper south windows. I
imagined that God was singling me out to receive this message
from heaven, and that he was glad to see me. Although after the
first two grades we no longer attended Catholic school, we still
attended Mass every Sunday and Holy Day. Sometimes we
attended a High Mass, which in my memory lasted long hours,
officiated by Archbishop Edwin Byrne. He was white-haired and
bespectacled and had a kindly air about him. Dressed in elegant
red silk robes, he resembled royalty. As children, we didn't know
whether to genuflect or bow, so most of the time after Mass we
just stood on the sidelines watching awkwardly, fascinated as people from every walk of life clamored to be near him, to touch his
hand and kiss his ring. On many occasions I watched as my parents stood in line in front of the cathedral steps. My father would
remove his hat and kneel before the archbishop as he gently kissed
the gold ruby ring on his right hand.

Although religion played a major role in our lives, it was
sometimes confusing. At St. Francis Parochial School, we were
required to learn prayers by repeating them over and over until
we could recite them without faltering. But I never grasped the
true meaning of what I was saying. "Hail Mary, full of grace"
didn't mean as much to me then as it does today. Since our parents weren't particularly well-off, each of us was allowed to
attend Catholic school only long enough to make our First Holy
Communion, which usually occurred in the second grade. We
were then enrolled in Wood-Gormley Elementary School, a few
blocks from home, where religion and prayers were nonexistent.
Sitting in church on Sundays became more difficult at this age
because attendance at daily Mass was no longer required, and
Sundays were a long seven days apart. A child could forget a lot
in those seven days. We no longer attended Mass on Holy Days

St. Francis Cathedral, 1950s. Photo courtesy Joseph E. Valdes.

of Obligation because that involved arriving late at school and required a written excuse from our parents. I imagine my understanding of church doctrine would be very different today had I remained in Catholic school.

The church changed radically as years passed, as did my understanding. For whatever reason, I didn't completely comprehend what Holy Mass was about, and it was hard to pay attention to the pomp and proceedings. Sitting next to our parents, we weren't allowed to move, talk, squirm, slouch, fall asleep, or even look behind us at the choir singing in the background. The dictates and rules handed down by the Vatican didn't noticeably affect me because it was in a country far, far away. As a child it seemed as though by the time I memorized one of the long and difficult prayers, someone came along and changed it. I still have difficulty remembering the newer version of the "Apostles' Creed" without referring to a prayer book; my brain has the old version deeply embedded in its crevices. As I look back, I realize that as a child, I understood very little about God and the Church. I only knew it was a big part of our lives and it was there to stay, and I obediently followed my parents' examples, whether I understood or

St. Francis Cathedral interior, 1950s. Courtesy New Mexico State Records
Center and Archives, Department of Tourism Collection No. 7849.

not. It wouldn't be until many years later that I would begin a
journey into understanding the mysteries of Catholicism.

Back then, it seemed as though everyone in our neighborhood
was deeply religious, from the elderly to the newly born, the latter
by proxy since babies received the Sacraments of Baptism shortly
after birth and Confirmation a few years later. This is what I knew
and I had no opinion of other religions because I assumed every
person of Spanish descent was Catholic. On a summer day in 1958,
as I walked around downtown Santa Fe, I happened onto a building with a sign that read "Spanish Baptist Mission." Naïve as it
may sound, I couldn't believe that a religion other than
Catholicism actually existed, especially one catering to Spanish-
speaking people. Although the occasion never arose, we wouldn't
have been allowed to enter churches other than our own, and this
building didn't even resemble a church; it looked just like any
other ordinary building. I didn't know what a Spanish Baptist *was*,
I just knew it *wasn't* a Catholic.

Bobby, First Holy
Communion, with
Jimmy, 1942.

As we grew to be teenagers, attending Sunday Mass became
more of a drudge, but I tried to be there because I still feared
burning in hell if I wasn't. An untimely divorce early in my
twenties made me believe I wasn't welcome. I never received an
official letter, but sermon after sermon indicated that divorced
Catholics were automatically excommunicated and could no
longer receive the Sacraments. Over the past thirty years, primarily because of my religious art and an annulment of that early
marriage, I have come full circle, embracing Catholicism and
gaining a new devotion to the Holy Spirit. It has been a journey
to relearn and participate in my religion. These days, I rarely
begin the day without a short prayer asking that my work be
infused with God's spirit. It is something my dad taught me a
number of years ago and I still practice it.

Chapter Six

OF SNOW AND WONDER
AND CHRISTMAS

The winters of my childhood were long and bitterly cold, with temperatures dropping many degrees below zero and snowdrifts piling up almost to the rooftops, or at least it seemed that way. Heavy snow weighed tree branches down, almost to their cracking point. Firewood was stacked to the ceiling in Uncle Joe's woodshed to our right or against the walls of the Martínez house next door. Mangy dogs searched for shelter outside anywhere they could find it. Neighborhood children stared out wistfully from the frost-painted windows, hoping that just thinking about it could stop the endless snow so they could venture out to play. Even in the wintertime, hardwood floors in our house glistened with a recent coat of oil, and the rag rugs on which we sat near the warm kitchen stove were faded from their weekly washing.

In the early years when I was in grade school, as Christmas day approached a freshly cut pine tree decorated with blue and green electric lights and popcorn garlands graced the living room. Sometime in the early 1950s, this decorated tree was replaced by a table-top tree made of tin or plastic, dotted with small decorations. This change disappointed us because Christmastime was supposed to be magical. Eventually I would learn the reason for this change, and it had nothing to do with not being good children.

At some point I discovered that Dad was never interested in Christmas; it was just another day for him. As children, of course, we looked forward to Christmas with great joy and anticipation. Dad didn't share this enthusiasm, although he helped Mom bring in a tree every year. He had been brought up in a strict environment, and there must not have been a focus on Christmas, at least not on the commercial aspect. The religious celebration was always at the forefront of his life growing up, highlighted by Christmas Eve Mass, special foods, and sacred music. My father's family thought Christmas trees were gringo affectations, designed to generate sales for the newly established general stores. (The Sears catalog was a dream book, filled with notions and merchandise that didn't fit into Santa Fe's style, at least not on West Houghton Street.) If gifts were given, it was throughout the year, a rocking horse; a small, red wagon; a doll; or a wooden toy. If Christmas gifts were purchased, they were limited to necessities.

When my mother was growing up in Ojo de la Vaca, her family didn't celebrate a Christmas that involved Santa Claus and brightly wrapped gifts either, since daily survival was enough of a challenge. They focused instead on the simpler side of Christmas, food and church. But as my parents settled into domesticity, my mother looked forward to this holiday. Within twelve years Mother had given birth to six children, and she attempted to imprint her love for the season on us, including the traditions and food.

During those years, we always had a beautiful, fresh pine tree that sat in the living room on a homemade wooden stand. Even though gifts were meager, at least we had a sense of Christmas and the joy surrounding it, represented by a beautifully decorated tree with multicolored glass balls and big red and green lights that illuminated the dark winter nights. I loved being outside at night, watching the lights sparkling through the window.

For whatever reason, one Christmas Eve, after having too much to drink, Dad picked up the tree, lights and all, and sent it flying out into the middle of the snow-blanketed yard. Rosalie and I stood by and watched, holding each other's hands. The following day, we helped Mother gather up the strings of lights and place them in a paper sack. It was the last time there was ever a big, decorated Christmas tree in our house.

Nevertheless each of us received at least one Christmas gift, usually homemade, but once in a while Santa Claus would visit, bearing gifts that made our eyes light up. One year, my seven-year-old sister Rosalie unwrapped a small porcelain tea set. Tiny cups and saucers decorated with little blue flowers barely filled the palm of her hands. She lovingly carried it down the street for Cousin Teresa to admire, and in her haste and excitement stumbled in the driveway and the precious tea set went flying. She came home in tears, holding the broken pieces in her hands.

My Christmas wishes never came true, so I had a difficult time believing in Santa Claus. When I was seven, I spent several months begging and praying for a piano. My biggest fantasy was that if Santa brought a beautiful piano, I could certainly play melodies that would captivate audiences all over the world. No matter how much I begged, there was never a piano sitting in the living room on Christmas morning. Instead, I'd find a sweater, or socks, or whatever else Mom could scrape together that year. I have no idea where this piano fixation emerged from, since the only one I would have been exposed to was in the music room at school, and we weren't allowed to touch it. I imagine that had my wish ever come true, the piano would have eventually sat in a corner gathering dust, since I was never able to read music.

At school we exchanged names and gave and received inexpensive gifts. An affordable gift for us to give was a LifeSavers book. These were multicolored, book-shaped, thin cardboard boxes filled with different flavored rolls of LifeSavers candy. We didn't put a lot of thought into these gifts, which probably cost less than a dollar, and I was never sure they were appreciated by the person who received them, but they were affordable. I searched my classmates' faces for some glance or sign of approval, but it never came—they quickly unwrapped my humble offering and shoved it in a corner until the class party was over and usually proceeded to fawn over perfume given to them by a best friend. Mother always asked how the party went, and I would put on a happy face and describe all the neat presents everyone received and add a white lie, claiming my classmate liked her LifeSavers as I cradled the small plastic nothing I had received.

The truly special moments of Christmas didn't involve gifts, but rather the sharing of time together. These moments were forever impressed in our hearts by the lighting of luminarias, or bonfires (not to be confused with the paper lanterns also known as luminaries or *farolitos*). Snow was cleared from the edges of the driveways closest to the street. Wood was chopped into sticks about two feet long and stacked in crisscross layers until they reached a height of about three feet. The stack of kindling was then lit and everyone gathered around to keep warm. In the dark, still nights, the crackling sound of burning wood and the fiery patterns made by the flying embers were truly gifts from heaven. Long after we'd gone to bed, my brothers returned from Midnight Mass and stood near the fire, exchanging stories until the wee hours of the morning. To entertain themselves, they lit long sticks of wood, which they waved in every direction as the tip burned down, creating designs in the air that stood out in the dark, magically filling the area with red and yellow waves of light. As the last coal burned down and the chill attacked their uncovered ears, they raced quickly up the driveway to the house, waved goodbye to their friends, entered quietly, and crawled sleepily into bed.

I've never liked the wintertime, perhaps because I wasn't often allowed to play outside in the snow. Or maybe it's because we walked two miles to school every day from the time I was six years old. I laugh as this recollection comes to mind, because I wonder how many times children all over the country have rolled their eyes at their parents' and grandparents' claims about trudging so many miles in waist-high snow. But it was true, and God, I hated that cold walk. It didn't matter if there were two feet of snow; we had no choice but to face the elements. In those days, schools were rarely closed because of snowfall. Sometimes we weren't much taller than the snowdrifts piled high along the roads or leaning heavily against the houses. Most days we arrived at school frozen to the core with wet socks and shoes stuck to our frozen feet and wet mittens stuck to our fingers. Even when we were lucky enough to wear galoshes, the snow somehow slipped into the tops of our boots. As a child I believed that there should be a law that school was only open on nice sunny days.

We grew up poor, with seven kids and only one car, which Dad drove to work, and we walked everywhere we went (mostly school and church), and then we walked some more. The Martínez family next door drove their kids to school every day in a big station wagon—nice, warm, and cozy. They passed us by almost every day, steam clouds billowing from the exhaust, tires noisily crunching the snow packed on the street. Except for an occasional lift—once a year or so, we watched as the car slowly disappeared around the corner. The temperature might plummet to ten degrees below zero and they still drove right past us as though we were invisible, all eyes looking forward. And we did the same, heads pulled down into our scarves and hats, so as not to appear too anxious for a ride or too disappointed if we didn't get one. Not getting a ride was no excuse for being late, so we shuffled along at a quick pace.

Eleuterio Martínez was a well-educated, hardworking family man who worked for the county and later the post office, and he and his wife Frances were raising ten children. And, of course, most of them were in school at the same time and there was barely enough room in that station wagon for all of them. But we didn't care. We were young, and we were cold, and we didn't think about the space available in the warm car. We assumed they could simply open the door and stuff us in a warm crevice somewhere near the back.

Later on when we were teenagers, winter travel could be easier and more exciting, especially for the boys. Standing by the side of the road, they would bend down and pretend to tie their shoes so unsuspecting drivers wouldn't think they were up to something. Then they would grab onto the bumper of a slow-moving car and slide all the way to town, returning the same way. This went on for hours, and occasionally a disgruntled driver would stop his car, get out, and holler obscenities at the boys, threatening to call the police. Feigning repentance, they walked around the corner until that car was out of sight, and then resumed their activities. A favorite spot for sledding on a tire tube or makeshift sled was Gildersleeve Hill, which sloped from the top of the street all the way down into the parking lot next to Harrington Junior High. Everyone gathered there on snowy days before the school bell rang and immediately after school. It was a thrill for them to slide quickly down the hill, attempting to gain enough speed to propel them all the way to the end.

Chapter Seven

LANGUAGE AND PREJUDICES

Every one of the neighborhood children was bilingual, probably from the first words we spoke. My parents both spoke English. Dad worked for the Forest Service and then as a carpenter, so it was necessary for him to have a working command of both languages. We also lived in National City, California, for a time during World War II, when our parents worked for Rohr Aircraft, so speaking two languages was second nature to them both. During that time they spoke Spanish with families from our neighborhood who had also gone to California and English with people from other parts of the country. We lived in a government housing project while Dad worked in the factory heat-treating aluminum to make it hard. Mother mixed paint to finish airplanes. On weekends the families gathered in Chula Vista for picnics, where, after speaking English all week, it was a delight to listen to the music and language of our culture, which remained far away in Santa Fe until the end of the war.

At home in Santa Fe, the older boys had their own gangs, *las gavillas*, small groups of same-aged friends and relatives from our street, Don Cubero, and Calle Grillo Streets. They also hung around with their gringo friends, Anglos who lived down the street, Jimmy Stingler and Charles Bryant (who earned the name Piojo after a bout of head lice). As a group, they spoke English to each other and Spanish to those who understood, and eventually they taught each other and us to speak both languages, adding to the instruction we had at home. By the fourth grade, we spoke a mixture of Spanish and English, popularly called Spanglish, and we moved easily in and out of one or the other, sometimes fracturing both. Some in the group understood a little Spanish but couldn't pronounce the words, so when they spoke, words took on a whole new meaning. This was referred to as *mocho*, indicating the word was pronounced incorrectly, but was close enough to get the message across and occasionally evoked gales of laughter.

Although a 1930 government census says otherwise, Grandma Romero spoke very little English. We had to speak Spanish in her presence, especially if the conversation was important, such as when we asked for a nickel to go to the store. Years before, Grandpa learned English on his various jobs. Grandma tried, but since it wasn't a priority in her life, she mastered only a few words that were useful for answering the telephone, like *hello*, *he's not home*, *thank you*, and *goodbye*. Spanish remained her language of choice.

Language discrimination probably existed in our public schools, but as children, my sister and I didn't notice it. My brothers remember it being an ongoing issue. Bobby often said that as soon as the teachers saw the brown color of his skin, or noticed his last name or the way he was dressed, he was singled out and embarrassed as often as possible. At Harrington Junior High, Emilio remembers being in the principal's office, complaining of a sore throat and asking for permission to go home. Mr. Walsh tersely commented that it was "those damn piñon nuts you Mexicans eat" that created the sore throat, and said Emilio would have to stay in school until it was dismissed. These incidents made us realize that if we were truly ill, we might as well stay home, because some teachers weren't sympathetic and insinuated we were faking. If learning problems existed, no one seemed to think they might be language-related, because in Catholic school you didn't pass to the next grade unless you could speak English clearly, and you had a set of sore knuckles to prove it.

Over the years I sensed a subtle difference in the way teachers interacted with Anglo students and Spanish-surnamed students. In high school, the history teacher didn't express his prejudice with words but found ways to exclude lower- and middle-class Spanish kids from discussions. Some of the Anglo students met with him during lunch hour and after school to discuss current world affairs and map out their participation in activities. In the eleventh grade, the history class listened to the lectures and took notes, hoping to get enough questions right to earn a passing grade. Only a select few were chosen to spend time discussing subjects such as Communism, war, and politics in general, subjects that didn't come up for discussion at our dinner table. It didn't really matter to us that none of us were given this privilege, since we were lucky if we survived history class at all. We couldn't imagine anyone wanting to spend time after hours at school, but it still bothered us to be singled out for exclusion.

For the most part, I didn't have Anglo *friends*, only *acquaintances*. Most of the Spanish kids banded together, and even though we didn't speak Spanish to each other, there was a silent recognition that we belonged to the same group. Some of us were embarrassed by our clothing, the way we spoke, and even what we ate. Often I would hear others referred to as, "You know, the little *Mexican* girl," where no distinction was made between being Spanish or being Mexican. Some people considered Mexicans to be inferior to Spaniards and would refer to members of both groups as Mexicans in a derogatory manner.

In junior high, my brother Jimmy was interested in an attractive blond classmate and began to spend time with her in between classes. One time he was unceremoniously shoved against a metal locker by a gym teacher who told him Mexicans weren't good enough to be holding the hands of Anglo classmates. Apparently the teacher made no cultural distinction in his case.

My cultural embarrassment began to spread to my sack lunch, which usually contained some sort of leftover meat or beans wrapped in a tortilla. I believed that all eyes were on me

as I enjoyed my tortillas. At first, I thought I was only imagining this. But it was as though a flashing red arrow pointed to my
mouth with the words, *tortilla eater*. I don't remember ever seeing any of the Anglo kids eating tortillas, at least not in public.
(Unlike in restaurants today, where tortillas are considered
authentic Mexican food, and a meal isn't considered a meal
without one.) There were more than a few times I was asked,
what *is* that you're eating, followed by a distasteful frown.
Eventually I started walking home for lunch where I could eat
tortillas to my heart's content, without scrutiny.

Prejudice affected local Spanish people when I was older as well.
As a recent high school graduate, I got a job in a bank. While
working as a clerk, I couldn't help but notice the treatment of
Spanish people. We had two hometown banks: Santa Fe
National Bank and the First National Bank. Unlike today, the
low-level employees were all local Spanish people for the most
part. The president and all the officers were locals too, but were
mostly Anglo, with the exception of one Spanish junior vice
president who rose to the rank of officer from the working class,
an unusual case since many employees stayed at one position
for several years without promotions.

The banks were always willing to mortgage a house for a
loan as small as $500, and many Spanish families in the poorer
neighborhoods relied on them to do just that. If the payments
weren't paid promptly and the loan fell behind, the bank referred
the account to the Santa Fe Credit Bureau to take action, and
take action they did. The credit bureau would telephone, stop by
work or home, garnish wages, harass, and use every tactic at
their disposal to assure payment was collected, regardless of the
person's circumstances. St. Vincent's Hospital also followed this
practice when an expensive medical emergency wasn't paid up
within a few months. Most blue-collar Spanish families didn't
have health insurance, so my father's stomach surgery in the
mid-1950s cost thousands of dollars that our family couldn't
afford to pay except in small increments. For a number of years
I watched my parents field the constant pressure for payment,

even though they did their best to pay the bank and hospital on time. The long periods of unemployment during Dad's illness did nothing to help an already stressful situation. Many working-class families had their credit rating ruined by frivolous lawsuits filed by the credit bureau. Its interference made it impossible for families to buy cars, appliances, or other items without going to finance companies that charged excessive interest rates and carrying charges. A fifty-dollar payment reduced the debt by only a few dollars each time. My parents' credit history consisted of small hospital and doctor bills, which even after they were paid remained on their record to haunt them up to their retirement many years later.

Chapter Eight

HAIRCUTS AND OTHER HARROWING EXPERIENCES

On the day I was born, Grandma Inés came to see me, and she asked Mom why she had dabbed Mercurochrome all over my tiny head. At birth I had curly, bright red hair and a freckled nose, and my grandmother tried to wash the color off when she first bathed me. Twelve years later, when I was in seventh grade, I had not yet had a haircut. As a result, my thick red hair reached down beyond my waist, and the braids were wide and heavy. The rare trip to the local carnival in the summertime was an uncomfortable occasion since my favorite ride was the Ferris wheel, and the weight of my hair yanked my head back as we circled skyward. Since I couldn't easily look up, I usually ended up getting dizzy. I also suffered from frequent headaches that Mother attributed to the length and weight of my hair. I watched with interest as my sister Rosalie sat quietly while Mother regularly trimmed her straight black hair. A few wisps snipped here and there and she was off. Enduring not only the daily discomfort but also the time-consuming ritual of having my hair braided, at some point I decided it was time for my first haircut. After all, I was almost a teenager. However, no amount of begging and cajoling convinced my parents of this necessity. Mother gently assured me that if it were not for my father, I would have had a haircut already.

I considered it a curse to be the only redhead for several generations in our family and never understood why my hair was never to be cut. Was I being saved for some sacrificial ritual reserved only for redheaded children? Eventually, perhaps because of my constant begging, it was finally decided that I would, at long last, get the haircut I had dreamed of for so many months. I imagined sitting in the beauty parlor, sporting a head full of suds during the shampoo; the beautician, a tall woman with skin like porcelain, elegantly coiffed hair, and long red nails, would skillfully and expertly trim and shape my hair. It would then be wound in wire brush rollers, and I would read the latest ingénue magazine while under the hair dryer, emerging stylish and fashionable. The week dragged on, and in great anticipation I counted the hours. No longer would I look like Pippi Longstocking, braids crowning my head, interlaced with ribbons that cascaded down the sides. (My mother had expertly braided my hair for years, but how many different ways could you decorate someone's head?) The day finally arrived, and I couldn't contain my excitement. I was up far too early and waited patiently while my dad shaved, showered, dressed, and ate breakfast. My mother insisted on braiding my hair for the last time, one thick braid with a wide yellow ribbon tied at the end.

It was ten o'clock by the time we rode down our street in the maroon 1948 Ford four-door sedan, and then, of course, we stopped to gas up a few blocks later on Galisteo Street. As we headed toward town, I relived my entry into the world of beauty parlors and glamour, which lasted until we parked the car on a side road near the plaza and walked a short distance. My dad directed me through a doorway of the DeVargas Hotel. I spotted four or five chairs, and after I sat in one, a barber came over and slipped a piece of tissue around my neck, over which he snapped a striped cotton cloth and arranged it over my body. This was to keep hair from falling on my clothes, he explained, and, scissors in hand, with one quick motion, he snipped the braid off. He then asked my dad if he wanted to save the twenty inches or so of hair, so they unceremoniously tucked the braid in a bag, with ribbon still attached, removed the cloth from my shoulders, brushed me off a bit, and my dad paid the tab. I remember looking at him and noticing tears in his eyes as we quickly headed toward the car.

I sat quietly the entire trip home, facing the window so Dad wouldn't see any tears. I was still in shock when we arrived home, clutching the bag with my now precious hair. I looked like a Dutch girl with a bad haircut; I now had a pyramid-shaped head, like someone whose edges had been sheared with pinking shears. I couldn't face my mother, and I'm not sure what she thought, since I walked straight into the bathroom and collapsed onto the rug, still clutching the bag holding my braid. I sobbed in disbelief. I couldn't understand what had happened; this was supposed to be a day filled with great promise, not sorrow. It would be hours before I felt strong enough to move around. I sat at the kitchen table, trying to smile and act like everything was fine. I hadn't known I was going to a barbershop, not a beauty shop, and I didn't know how to tell them this.

About a week later my mother suggested that perhaps a home permanent would be the solution. After all, a few more curls around my already wavy head wouldn't hurt. I could have averted disaster, but I didn't know any better. That weekend, as I sat in a chair near the kitchen table, I participated in the ritual of the Toni Home Permanent: a pink and white cardboard box filled with bright pink plastic curlers, cotton balls, smelly solution, and promises of beautiful curls. According to the box, featuring a woman with springy brown curls adorning her face, a set of these lovely curls would soon be mine. I arranged the contents, a comb, and a plastic bowl neatly in a row. For a moment, there was hope that I might somehow be transformed...by the time the rollers were removed from my hair, I had a strange feeling I would never forget this day. And I was right. A few hours later I was no longer the Dutch girl—adorning my head were hundreds of tight, frizzy, corkscrew curls, pointing in every direction and guaranteed to make me a laughingstock.

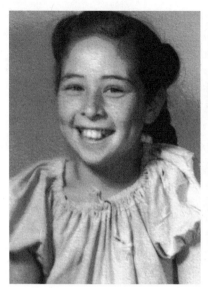

Before and after the infamous haircut incident, 1950s.

Again, I smiled weakly at Mom, assuring her how much I liked it, because I didn't want to hurt her feelings, hoping that somehow I would survive this latest horror. After all, I had already endured the stares and (I imagined) pointing fingers and whispers at school after the haircut; surely I could endure reactions from this new but exaggerated Shirley Temple look. For about a week, my only consolation was watching my favorite television programs, immersing myself in daydreams about the Cisco Kid and his sidekick Pancho. I knew school soon would be over, and that was my other consolation.

Admittedly, I didn't own the monopoly on bad haircuts. My brothers endured what they considered a far greater torture than I could imagine, and far more often. Every few weeks, Dad would take out the notorious metal clippers and the infamous can of 3-in-1 Oil, with which he would lubricate all the moving and nonmoving parts of the electric clippers. There was no escape. One by one, Emilio, Jimmy, and Bobby were marched into the kitchen. They sat at the edge of the table and grimaced as a towel was placed around their shoulders. Under threat of severe punishment, each one was instructed to sit still. The strong metallic smell of the oil permeated the room as Dad generously reapplied it to the blades, oblivious to the fact that much of it spread over the boys' heads as he clipped.

With tensed shoulders and closed eyes, Jimmy winced as the clippers rode noisily across his head. He let out a howl as they nipped at his ear, for which he received a quick rap on the head and an admonition from Dad to be still. The metal teeth traversed the entire diameter of his head, leaving about a pound of hair on the floor. Thankfully, the episode was finally over, and he stepped up to the mirror to inspect the damage as he dusted himself off. (We still tease my brothers about their haircuts, intimating that Dad would place a medium-sized mixing bowl that we called the "number three" over their heads, and then would trim whatever excess hair was below the rim of the bowl.) Although the smell of oil lingered a few more days, the ordeal was soon forgotten . . . until the next time.

Along with monthly haircuts, our parents also conducted periodic head lice checks. These nasty little critters, more popularly known as *piojos*, spread from child to child like wildfire, and the only cure was affected by smearing a thick, black, foul-smelling grease over the entire head. There was no telling how difficult the removal process of this goop would be after the lice were gone a few days later. Every so often the homeroom teacher called the school nurse to the classroom and whispered something. They exchanged *tsk, tsk* looks, and one of the kids would be carted off to the nurse's office, sent home, and instructed not to return for at least a week. Sometimes there was an epidemic, usually involving five or six good friends, and they all would be taken out of school together. And we silently wondered, *Hey, what about us?* We wanted a vacation too, but our parents never were forced to grease our heads, no matter how often we insisted that there were imaginary bugs all over our hair. That ploy never seemed to work.

Chapter Nine

NEIGHBORHOOD PETS

Most everyone in our neighborhood had a favorite pet, even though the standing joke was that if your dog was missing for more than a day, someone had probably made him into tamales! There was never a request to "let the dog out," because the dog was always out. Pets were meant to live outdoors, period. Besides, no mother in her right mind was going to allow a dog to be potty trained on her newly waxed hardwood floors.

Grandma Romero had an old, shaggy crossbred mutt named Gizmo. He was a German shepherd-Great Dane-collie mix. Not only was he old, but he was half-blind and had multicolored fur that was so matted on one side, it made him appear to walk unevenly. Though included in many family photos, Gizmo spent most of his days lying in the doorway of Grandma's porch and never moved unless he knew it was dinnertime. He wasn't much fun to play with, as it seemed he never had enough energy even to wag his tail. The dog was about fifteen years old when I was a child, and one day we just didn't see him anymore.

Emilio, Grandma and Grandpa Romero, Rudy (kneeling), Gizmo, and cousin Josephine.

Our dog King was special. He was our consummate protector, and strangers feared him. A shiny black Doberman pinscher, he chose Jimmy as his master. King followed him to Harrington Junior High each morning and then slept in the backseat of an old abandoned car in the vacant lot next door. When the dismissal bell rang, King would jump out of the car and sit patiently next to the flat front tire, waiting until Jimmy showed up so they could walk home together. Dogs wandered freely around the neighborhoods without a leash, and King was no exception.

On Saturday afternoons, King followed Jimmy to the movie theater, sitting outside in the shade until the movie was over. The postman wouldn't deliver mail to our house any time he spotted King nearby, but instead left it at Grandma's house across

the street. Unfortunately, even in those supposedly more innocent times, some ill-intentioned people didn't particularly like
animals. Someone fed King poisoned meat, and when we saw
him suffering, we put him in the backseat of the car and rushed
toward the vet's office. He didn't make it, but we never forgot
how loyal and loving he had always been. A few months later he
was replaced by a smaller dog, a beagle mix named Peewoh, who
made up in noise what he lacked in size. Peewoh was more
Mom's dog, since Jimmy wasn't about to get as close to this one
as he had been to King. (Even today, Jimmy doesn't own a dog.)

Occasionally mean, cranky dogs became obstacles on our
walk to school. We quickly learned which dogs would allow you
to walk past without incident and which ones you needed to
avoid, either by walking on the other side of the street, finding
an alternate route, or carrying a hefty stick and hoping the dog
would be intimidated enough to leave you alone. We always had
a Plan B, since we knew some of these unruly dogs came flying
out to the street any time we passed near their houses, and their
owners didn't seem to care whether it frightened us or not. On
many occasions stray dogs would attack the chickens in our
yards and those of the neighbors. These dogs would sometimes
end up being disposed of by a bullet from a .22 rifle, a necessary
solution to a problem that was depleting the chicken population
and depriving some people of their food.

Dogs weren't always the only obstacles, though. Every so
often I cut through the Martínez yard next door and took a
short-cut that landed me near the end of West Houghton where
it connected to Galisteo Street. One morning, I sauntered
through their yard, thinking of nothing more than the amount of
time I had to reach Wood-Gormley School before the first bell
rang and how many steps I could cut off my record from the previous day. I reached up and casually grabbed a handful of seeds
and leaves from the elm tree and carefully dropped them behind
me, one by one, marking my path (in case I got lost, I could find
my way home, just like in the movies). I spread the seeds like a
flower girl in a wedding dropping rose petals with each step,
oblivious to everything around me. Suddenly, a sharp pain in the
palm of my hand rudely awakened me from my daydream.

Puzzled, I looked down to see Tío Fortino's old banty rooster jamming its beak into my hand, apparently thinking that whatever I had in my hand was rooster food. I let out a howl and took off running, but he chased me for more than a block, pecking at my heels, even though I had dropped the seeds five hundred feet back. I didn't take that shortcut again and hoped that someday that cranky rooster would end up in someone's soup pot.

Chapter Ten

THE PICTURE BOX AND OTHER ENTERTAINMENT

There wasn't much to do in the summertime, since *vacation* simply meant no school for three months. Our family never left Santa Fe, or even the neighborhood. We never expected to be taken anywhere, and it never happened. I was so used to staying close to home, I didn't travel to Albuquerque, only sixty miles away, until I was in my twenties, and didn't visit Taos until my thirties. The required "what I did on my summer vacation essay" was the same every year...nothing. That is, until television made its debut.

It was 1951 and we all held our breaths as Dad cut open an oversized box he had just carried into the house. I remember the look of pride on his face, as Jimmy helped carry it into the living room. He was doing something wonderful for his children. It turned out to be a great day, a genuine treat, and our Christmas present for the next few years even if it wasn't Christmas: a big television set in a boxy, yellow-hued wooden cabinet. It said

RCA all over the box, and the boys unpacked it carefully, know-ing the box would make a great fort for the younger kids. A long, heavy metal pole antenna was attached to the side of the house with large metal clamps and screws and extended about six feet beyond the edge of the roof. When there was static on the screen, one of us had to step outside and slowly turn the metal pole until the signal from Albuquerque was aligned and the static cleared up.

From the start, I loved television (even when it didn't come with a remote control). When I was alone, I sat with only a few inches between me and the screen, taking it all in. (I'm told this is one of the reasons I needed to wear eyeglasses by the time I was thirteen.) The weekly fare played primarily in the after-noons and evenings: *The Cisco Kid*, *Tom Mix*, *Hopalong Cassidy*, *The Ed Sullivan Show*, *Zorro*, and local programming from Albuquerque on Channel 7. *The Dick Bills Show* intro-duced a young country singer named Glen Campbell to us. (I remember wondering years later why he never mentioned his years at our little television station in the mountains of New Mexico. That was the closest we ever came to having a real celebrity in our midst.) I believe television was an escape out of the life I led. A lot was going on in our family, problems with Bobby's behavior and the like, over which I had absolutely no control, but it didn't keep me from feeling the effects. I spent a lot of time worrying about school, grades, family squabbles, my perception of poverty, etc. I thought my life was normal, but the inside of the TV set was filled with fun, adventure, romance... I was hooked. I rushed home after school to watch as many pro-grams as I could fit in before dinnertime. I could draw the Indian motif from the test pattern as I sat in school daydreaming of what I would watch that afternoon. I read the fifteen-cent *TV Guide* from cover to cover, perusing the day's schedule, vaguely interested in tidbits about the actors and their lives. It was a let-down when the programming was over for the night and the tired strains of "The Star-Spangled Banner" played.

Our parents watched some programs, and we sat quietly waiting for them to be over. These included dramas that they never saw at the movies, because they never went. My father's favorite was the *Gillette Cavalcade of Sports'* Friday Night Fight, featuring such great boxers as Kid Gavilan and Carmen Basilio. They rarely missed watching *Life is Worth Living*, a Catholic program hosted by Bishop Fulton J. Sheen. He was the first "televangelist," and by today's standards, he would be a minor leaguer. Every week we gathered in the living room to listen to him speak of Catholicism, family values, and virtues. He had a flamboyant nature and his bishop's garb flowed like fine taffeta with each movement. My parents listened intently as he covered a wide range of subjects, standing next to a blackboard, his trusty piece of white chalk in his hand, writing in a beautiful, readable script, loudly dotting I's, crossing T's, and underlining words for emphasis. Most of the subjects he covered were over my head: Marx, Lenin, Stalin, and atheism, but I sat patiently, feigning interest, waiting for his theme song to herald the end of the program. Today, Bishop Sheen is a candidate for sainthood, and his programs are replayed regularly on Catholic television. After watching an old episode recently, I realized that his sermons were primarily based on common sense, and that he expressed opinions about life, war, and death, which at the time were controversial subjects to discuss on national television.

After school, my first stop was usually at the refrigerator, and the second was the living room where the television set sat next to the aluminum picture window. Early on there were only two channels, later to be joined by a third. In the evening, the *Loretta Young Show* was one of our family favorites. She had a certain way of gliding...no, floating...onto the stage, enveloped in layers of chiffon that undulated with her every move. Visiting our living rooms on a regular basis were the slapstick antics of Uncle Miltie, Edgar Bergen, and Pinky Lee, along with the adventures of Boston Blackie and Rin Tin Tin. And how we wished we could be the lucky ones to receive a million dollar cashier's check, courtesy of *The Millionaire*—how much candy and how many Cadillacs would that buy!

A few horror movies starring Vincent Price, Lon Chaney, and others managed to frighten me enough to cause a few sleepless nights. They told of dark and gloomy cemeteries, vampires, ghouls, and ghosts, subjects I knew little about. I made it a point to never watch these programs unless someone else was in the room, that way I could pretend to not be afraid. It is likely that these horror movies, which left much to the imagination, were partially responsible for my becoming such a scaredy-cat in my preteen years.

I can't say exactly when this began—an insidious cloud of fear that transformed me into a fearful child, not on the surface, but in the depths of my soul, where bogeymen and goblins waited at every corner once the sun set. Our neighborhood was crime-free year after year, so there was no real threat from outside forces. But I became afraid to walk home after sunset following a neighborhood game of baseball held a few blocks away. Vines and branches against dimly lit walls became invisible predators ready to pounce on me as I walked through the alleys and fields toward home. Sometimes I wouldn't budge until Jimmy walked me to a spot four hundred feet from the house, chastising me all the way for making him miss his turn at bat. From there I would fly as though propelled by a hurricane-strength tailwind into the safety and comfort of our adobe walls.

In the middle of the night when everyone else was asleep, I would peep through the curtains in our room into the street to make sure no strangers lurked there. Once as I was looking out, I swore I saw a tall, skinny man standing by the window. I crept into my parents' room and shook them awake with my news. Dad jumped out of bed, dived into his trousers, and went outside as I turned the porch light on. I hung onto my mother's arm, trembling in fear, but he came back in to say there was nothing there. In junior high there were times my friend Rosalena and I would overstay a visit at her house on Galisteo Street, about eight blocks from my neighborhood. On these occasions, she walked me halfway home, and then I would have to turn around and walk her half that distance back. Sooner or later we'd both take off running in the direction of our streets, and I'd arrive home, panting and out of breath, as though the devil himself was at my heels.

Television surely had contributed to this state I was in. I had never given much thought to cemeteries; they were just places of rest for the dearly departed and those not so dearly departed.

But the movies made them places of terror and horror, where the undead and risen dead walked around under a full moon in the pitch black of night, looking for innocent souls to devour. Ghostly bodies rose from carved granite headstones and floated through the air with the greatest of ease, and vampires smacked their lips as they zeroed in on a particularly worthwhile neck. I was an impressionable child, and through the power of television, I began to believe there were evil, scary things out there, not a pleasant discovery. To this day I have never forgotten an episode of a program whose name has long escaped me, perhaps *The Twilight Zone*, in which each night a man dreamt that a hand was grabbing his ankle as he slept. He would awaken covered with sweat, screaming at the top of his lungs. Assured by doctors that these were just nightmares, he attempted to go about his daily life as usual, but each night the dream returned. Somewhere along the line an X-ray was taken of his foot and it showed a skeletal hand firmly grasping his ankle. Fifty years later, I still recall the chill that ran through me as I watched the final minutes of the program. Other shows also etched themselves into the narrow pockets of my child-mind.

The families who appeared on television were foreign to us—they were all white, middle- or upper-class, and probably never saw a tortilla on their dinner tables. Naturally, no Spanish parents raising large families in a two-room house were shown. But, despite our vast differences, we faithfully visited these actors every week. It seemed so simple: just ask and you shall receive. Their existence seemed too easy—their days were filled with fun, love, and warmth. Everyone was smiling and happy. Even their school days passed without a struggle; everyone excelled without effort. There was no bigotry, no bias, no anger, no hardships, no alcohol, family squabbles, smoking, or pregnant teens. Everyone got along, the guy always got the girl, and everyone rode off into the sunset to live happily ever after. And we devoured it.

By 1956 television had become more refined. Now situation comedies were on, featuring Eve Arden as *Our Miss Brooks*, and Red Skelton, a tall and lanky clown-faced comedian whose pratfalls and backflips elicited wails of laughter from the home audience.

Also, a slew of advertising attempted to motivate everyone to keep up with the Joneses, or better still, with the Garcías. The ad for Plymouth automobiles let us know that "Good taste is never extreme," whatever that meant. Then there were *The Nelsons*, the family from middle America who represented everything we were not, but we could hope for. Howdy Doody, a freckle-faced wooden puppet, frolicked across the stage and the airwaves; Lucy and Ricky Ricardo attempted a mixed marriage; and other family dramas imitated life somewhere far, far away from our living rooms. Adlai Stevenson was defeated by Dwight D. Eisenhower, the Korean War was fought in a far-off land, and Santa Fe continued to be our island where doors remained unlocked, even at night, and children played without a warning about dangerous strangers.

Before television arrived in our uneventful lives, the important dramas were staged on local AM radio. Our Santa Fe stations, KTRC and KVSF, provided many programs that offered drama unlike anything we ever experienced. Every morning at exactly 10:30, the radio was switched on. This meant that Mom was unavailable for the next hour, so we'd better not need anything. She was about to be immersed in the soap operas of that decade: *Our Gal Sunday* and *The Romance of Helen Trent*. At that moment, the familiar strains of "Red River Valley" wafted through the air and the announcer's voice boomed through the kitchen, "Once again, we present *Our Gal Sunday*, the story of an orphan girl named Sunday from the little mining town of Silver Creek, Colorado..."

Sunday, our heroine, had married the handsome and wealthy Lord Henry Brinthrope. Day after day we heard the question, "Can this girl from the little mining town in the West find happiness as the wife of a wealthy and titled Englishman?" Along with Mom (and probably a large percentage of the women in Santa Fe), we were captivated by this rags-to-riches saga, every woman's dream of finding true love. Each day we waited in anticipation to see if Sunday and her royal husband would survive the clutches of the many wicked and wayward women who were thrown into his path. Any time I was home from school, I was never too ill to slip into the kitchen and listen to the latest episode, wrapped in a blanket and holding a cup of hot tea.

The Romance of Helen Trent followed immediately and was just as compelling. Her life was filled with romantic escapades, but she kept (I assumed) turning down suitors just in case her *real* true love would somehow drop out of the sky. It wasn't unusual for Mom (and sometimes even Dad) to urge, "*Andale,* Helen. Come on. This is the one. Don't give him up." We were always a little sad when one of these perfect men got away and thrilled when she realized, just in time, that she was falling for a jerk.

While most of the neighborhood women listened to these two soaps, teens also had their radio favorites, the *Inner Sanctum Mysteries,* and we were right there with them, mesmerized by their intensity. An ongoing mystery series that ran from 1941 to 1952, it aired each night, opening with the loud, eerie, unnerving sound of a creaking door. We were certain that once that door opened, something terrifying lurked behind it. About ten or twelve kids gathered to listen on Grandma Romero's front porch, where two extension cords stretched through the front door so we could all huddle around listening to the latest episode. These radio dramas were scheduled in the late evening, and after listening intently to the chilling intonations of the characters, some of us went straight home and slipped under the covers, *just in case.* Having survived the previous night without incident, we anxiously awaited the hour when the same scene would be repeated next evening. It was disappointing when the program went off the air, since it had provided us with an abundance of thrills and chills.

We also escaped from reality by going to the movies. There were four movie houses in Santa Fe: the Lensic, the El Paseo, and the Alley theaters, all owned by the Salmon Greer family, and later the Santa Fe Theater. Each Saturday morning at the downtown theater, they held contests that featured events from bubble gum blowing to naming the presidents. These took place during intermission and were looked forward to with great anticipation. Prizes awarded included some highly coveted plastic gizmo, Monopoly game, or stuffed animal. The Lensic Theater was located on the west side of downtown, next to the entrance to Burro Alley. Its name was derived from the first initials of the Salmon grandchildren's names: Lila, E. John, Nathan, Sara, Irene, and Charles. The Lensic was the most elegant place a barrio kid could enter, with its carved stone gargoyles high on the cornice peering malevolently down at us. The interior of the building was plush and exotic, its walls painted with colorful frescoes. The bathroom walls were lined with gleaming tile and mirrors against velvet-flocked wallpaper. The ceiling had a number of tiny lights embedded in it that resembled a night sky full of stars. There were more than eight hundred seats, and most of the time we tried to sit in the front rows.

Once the newsreel started, the whole theater became silent. This was followed by several cartoons, coming attractions, and the main feature. An occasional "follow-the-bouncing-ball" episode lasting about five minutes broke the entire theater into song. A few of us would sneak up to the mezzanine, climb the stairs up to the last row, right below the projector windows, and sit on the puffy, comfortable rocking seats, the entire theater in the expanse before us. We experienced unbelievable luxury as we stretched our legs and rested our feet on the seats of the row in front of us. That is, until the ushers flashed their lights in our faces and escorted us back downstairs where we belonged, to the delight of older teens sitting in the paid seats, hooting loudly and blowing rings of smoke toward the ceiling. At intermission we ran into the lobby, trying to be first in line to indulge in bags of freshly popped, buttered popcorn, bubbling Cokes, and boxes of candy. We watched movies featuring Flash Gordon, the Three Stooges, and our favorite, the Little Rascals. Ma and Pa Kettle movies played often, along with a musical featuring Jane Powell and Debbie Reynolds, *Hit the Deck*. Blockbusters such as *East of Eden* starring James Dean drew large crowds of teens and adults.

The El Paseo Theater was centrally located on San Francisco Street, next to the Chinese restaurant. In earlier days it was the Paris Theater. It, too, was luxurious but did not match the opulence of the Lensic. The Alley Theater was across from the Lensic. The facade of the one-story building was a fanciful attempt at mimicking the larger theater, but the interior was much like a big metal tunnel. Its fare was primarily Mexican movies aimed at the Spanish-speaking population, with such popular stars as Pedro Infante and Cantinflas, which I rarely went to see. My brothers recall that Infante was the most popular of the Mexican cowboys. He was not only handsome, but also a singer, romantic leading man, horseman, and comedian. I understood the language but found the plots less exciting than the rip-roaring movies presented by the other theaters. The Mexican comedians weren't nearly as funny to me as was Jerry Lewis. For the Saturday matinee at the Alley, we were treated to downright American Westerns, featuring the stars introduced to us through television: Roy Rogers, Hopalong Cassidy, the Lone Ranger, the Durango Kid, and Lash Larue, to name a few. We kept up with Tom Mix and followed the adventures of Red Ryder and his sidekick, Little Beaver.

In 1945 my brothers recalled it cost seven cents to get in, and the popcorn was five cents. By 1954 admission had increased to a quarter and popcorn was fifteen cents. For kids with empty pockets, the smell of freshly popped popcorn was a little hard to bear, but sometimes we managed to scrape up enough to enjoy a bag or two.

The Santa Fe Theater opened for business in the mid-1950s, and admission was twenty cents. It was located on Cerrillos Road right before Manhattan Street, a lot closer to home. Don Beers ran the theater, and he was always friendly to us, even though he knew we barely had enough money to buy a gumball. This theater also attempted to boost attendance by offering games and prizes. Each Saturday morning before the movie began, the emcee worked the crowd into a frenzy, and loud shouts of "Wahoo!" could be heard throughout the theater. Everyone arrived at the theater early enough to take part in the various contests, including a game loosely based on Bingo. The usual prizes were handed out to eager players, who bounded up on stage to receive these inexpensive tokens as though they'd never seen anything like them in their entire lives.

Although attending a movie was a great treat, it didn't happen often enough to suit us. We never attended movies during the week, or on Sundays, when the matinees featured what are now referred to as blockbuster movies, the ones the kids talked about at school. The price was only right on Saturday morning.

There wasn't much entertainment for the older neighborhood boys other than the movies, but they did look forward to wrestling matches held at the St. Michael's High School gym, which was next to the old cemetery where the PERA Building sits today. One of the wrestlers, Mike London, was a dark haired, goa-teed hulk of a man, featured along with another big wrestler, Gorilla Pogey. Following one of the matches, the name Pogey was tagged onto Louie Baca, one of the teens from their group, and eventually it stuck. The boys rarely had the price of admission. If they tried to sneak in, the security guards dragged them out and threatened them with major bodily harm if they returned.

Most people believed the wrestling matches were legitimate, but some claimed they were phony and that all the moves were rehearsed and choreographed. On one occasion when the boys finally scored enough small change to attend a match, State Policeman Happy Apodaca and a few of his buddies began boo-ing the wrestlers and calling them phonies. This continued through the match, and after it was over the wrestlers jumped out of the ring and confronted the hecklers with an offer to take them on any time they were ready. When the appointed time came, the wrestlers beat the locals soundly. Over the years, the matches gained new popularity and Mike London became a pro-moter after he retired from the ring. The matches were later tel-evised from Albuquerque on KOAT. The boys knew each wrestler by name and spent many hours imitating them, never again having to spend a dime to see them in person.

Chapter Eleven

SUM-SUM-SUMMERTIME

Our neighborhood wasn't half-bad in the summertime. We spent hours playing marbles in the dirt yard. Many prized steelies and cat's-eye marbles were forfeited to the collection of an unbeaten champ like my brother Jimmy, who confidently drew some lines onto the dirt with a small stick and nonchalantly cast his marbles into the center. In 1950 he was the marble champ of the whole neighborhood and of Harrington Junior High.

Jimmy had a bag of special marbles—shiny metal steelies, cat's-eyes, aggies, and the prized treasure, the *borraquio*, a fat marble about an inch and a half in diameter with swirls of bright color on its surface. Not quite round and a little rough, he guarded it like a diamond. Prized aggies were made from agate. Peewees were tiny glass marbles, the shooting of which had to be mastered since they were so small they prohibited accuracy without practice. Cat's-eyes were clear glass marbles with brightly colored plastic inserts that resembled a cat's eye. A steelie was a stainless-steel ball-bearing taken from automobile transmissions or wheels, about a half inch in diameter and a marble to respect if its owner mastered its use. Shot at just the right speed, it could crack an opponent's prized marble in half—or just as bad, chip and damage it.

At every opportunity, a group of boys (and sometimes girls) gathered around in the dirt yard at the top of our driveway, cloth bags of marbles in hand. Into the meticulously smoothed out dirt, Jimmy drew the "fats" (two half circles resembling a fish) with a center line through it, where each player placed a number of marbles depending on the size of the fats. The smaller the fats, the fewer marbles were placed inside it, thereby excluding a number of anxious players in early rounds and extending the playing time. Two lines were drawn in the dirt, and in order to participate in the game, you had to shoot a marble as close to the line as possible. This also established the shooting order. Each kid's turn involved knocking marbles out of the fats from the edge of a large circle drawn around it. The captured marbles became his, and he continued to shoot until he missed. The next kid would then take his turn. Whoever had the most marbles after the last one was knocked out was the winner. I had my own bag jangling with marbles I won from the boys and some pilfered from my brother's bag. But any time there was a serious game going, I was no match for my brother, who had the uncanny ability to hit a marble with such deadly accuracy as to knock it out of the fats without disturbing the other marbles. On the rare occasion that I made it past the first round, my joy was short-lived, as it wouldn't be long before I walked away with an empty bag.

Always looking for a way to make a quick nickel, each summer in the early 1950s my brother Bobby put on a carnival that included a talent show, usually held in one of the backyards, on a makeshift stage built from spare lumber gathered from the neighborhood. Frayed patchwork blankets propped up by long boards were held in place by large boulders and served as backdrops. Performances consisted of off-key singing and dancing, cartwheeling, and basic jumping up and down. Admission cost five cents and entitled you to a glass of Kool-Aid, but the glass had to be returned, since it belonged in one of the family cupboards.

Bernie, the eldest of the Gonzales girls from across the street, breezed onto the stage from behind the frayed curtains wearing a pink ballerina outfit, complete with tutu and well-worn ballet shoes. A rhinestone tiara and a "mink" coat completed the ensemble. We were easily impressed as we watched her attempt a pirouette standing on the tips of her toes because most of us had never seen a real ballet. As the show progressed, there were usually a few heart-stopping moments when an overzealous kid fell off a ladder or landed on his head attempting a full body flip. The loud wails generally produced a screaming mother to stop the show and send everybody home, whether they got their nickel's worth or not. But a few weeks later, it was showtime again.

Bobby was born to entertain; he was the ringmaster and wowed neighborhood kids with this backyard carnival, one nickel at a time. Between our house and Aunt Mela's he constructed rides from pieces of lumber found in backyards and alleyways. For example, once Bobby industriously dug a three foot hole in which he placed a five foot long pole protruding above ground for two feet. He then filled the hole with rocks and dirt. He drilled a hole in the center of a two-by-ten-inch piece of lumber, which he placed across the center of the pole, attached it with a large bolt, and then covered with a gob of grease. He nailed narrow slats of wood to serve as handles for the rider to hang on to. After the appropriate admission fee was paid, one kid would sit on each end and Bobby would stand in between, pushing from the side of the board until it gathered enough momentum to spin on its own, at which time he stepped out of the way. The ride lasted until the last full spin occurred.

Played in the middle of the road, neighborhood games of Kick the Can were as thrilling as any football game. Team members were chosen one at a time for each side, and the odd one who remained became the scorekeeper or water boy. These exciting head-to-head matches were interrupted only by occasional cars passing through the neighborhood that dispersed the players. After much cussing and fist waving, the competition resumed. The object of the game was to kick an empty can past the line into the other team's territory for a touchdown, and I imagine more pairs of already handed-me-down shoes were worn to the nub playing this game, since a lot of shuffling occurred as the dirt flew.

La Polvorita, old powder house on Galisteo Street. Photo courtesy
Historic Santa Fe Foundation.

One of our favorite play areas was on Galisteo Street, about
a block from our house next to a small stone building called La
Polvorita, an old powder house where the army once stored powder kegs in the 1860s. We imagined that cannons and cannon-
balls were stored inside, along with guns, rifles, and ammo, but
we were never strong or ingenious enough to break the lock or
push the door in, so the mystery remained. Besides, we didn't
want to get in trouble with the U.S. Army, as we imagined they
would arrest us for trespassing, so we were content to just play
with our make-believe weapons.

Every so often, newcomers to town set up living quarters
near our play area. We couldn't understand why they lived in
tents and slept on the hard ground. These vagabonds gathered
old lumber and constructed lean-tos against the walls of a building. They used the bathroom in the nearby bushes and brought
water from the acequias, irrigation canals where water was
released in premeasured amounts to each family along the system, for their cooking. When we told Uncle Willie that we
couldn't play there anymore because they had taken over the
whole area, he rode his Harley-Davidson motorcycle there,

Willie Romero on
Harley Davidson
Motorcycle, 1950s.

parked it in front of one of the tents, took his pistol out, and told
them to get the hell out. Dad explained that they were called
squatters, people who came from states like Oklahoma and
Kentucky, and if you didn't force them to move, they would
build shacks wherever they could get away with it. We never
saw them after that, but Uncle Willie said they probably set
camp on the other side of town and eventually assimilated into
the population.

During the rainy season, the acequias brimmed with water.
My dad's great-uncle, Tío Fortino, was in charge of the nearby
acequia that ran along the edge of his property and that of the
Apodacas, and also parallel to our street. The mother ditch, or
acequia madre, originated a long distance away near the upper
end of Canyon Road and traveled down Hickox Street, eventually arriving at our street and continuing down to the State

Penitentiary, where it ultimately served the gardens. From this main ditch, a small stream ran from Galisteo Street down through Houghton Street. At certain points the water was diverted to different neighbors as their turn came up. This irrigation system served our neighborhood gardens and also provided a bit of recreation for bored teenagers on hot summer afternoons. The sidewalk that ran along West Houghton from Galisteo Street was built over a culvert tunnel, and when you walked along this sidewalk your footsteps made a hollow sound. The boys would crawl more than one hundred feet through the tunnel from beginning to end when there was no water, emerging triumphantly at one end of the small concrete bridge on Galisteo Street.

The water in the acequia was crystal clear and had a layer of fine sparkling sand at the bottom. Horny toads flitted past the edges, taking cover under rocks and vegetation. Tío Fortino had a nice orchard on his property with apricot, apple, and peach trees, and among other things, grew great stalks of sweet corn in his garden. Dad and our neighbors used the water to irrigate our family vegetable gardens, which were grown in the large lot down the street that also served as our baseball field, although the water from the acequia couldn't travel to our gardens on its own. My brother Emilio assisted in diverting the acequia to serve this purpose by removing several bricks from the main diversion nearby, thus redirecting the flow to the crops planted in the open field (which is now part of my backyard on Lomita Street). When the watering was completed, the bricks were replaced and covered with a layer of dirt, averting any suspicion of tampering. We also used this water for household purposes, cooking and bathing, before indoor plumbing. A community well at the north side of the street next to Tío Fortino's house also served the neighborhood. It was an old stone well, and we used a bucket tied with a rope to haul water.

During the rainy season in mid-July, the arroyos filled with water and overflowed to create large ponds on the hill directly east of our house and across from Kika Martínez's pitched-roof house on Rosina Street. At this location, Jimmy, Cousin Junior, and the rest of the neighborhood boys spent days hauling rocks and logs to dam the culvert into one big pond, which served as a swimming hole. Cousin Junior recalled, "We spent most of the day gathering rocks and sticks and stacking them in a row on the edge of the culvert. One of us would tamp mud and leaves down to hold the rocks in place, while the others gathered different sized rocks. By the time the water started to pool, it was early afternoon and time for a swim. You wouldn't believe how much water we managed to divert; it was pretty deep. Anyway, I decided to dive in, and as I hit the cool water with a running jump, the momentum carried me to the bottom of the pond. There was a broken Coke bottle lodged between the rocks, and I dove right into it. I came out of the water fast, holding my bleeding hand. My cousin Emilio dragged me over to his bike and rode me home, where my mother applied a bandage. I didn't get to swim for a few days, but once it healed I was back there again. We started being more careful about gathering glass and sharp rocks before we built our dam."

The boys also tied long ropes to the branches of two large elm trees near the edge. Pretending to be Tarzan, they rode the rope across the short distance and catapulted themselves into the center of pond. Cloudbursts provided an added bonus when such abundant rain fell that we were able to wade in the pond every afternoon. The monsoon season usually started in mid-July and continued into August, but the pond primarily relied on the acequia water to keep it full.

The pleasures were often short-lived, however, since the damming was so effective that it kept water from reaching the State Penitentiary, located where Cordova Road and Cerrillos Road now intersect, about six blocks southwest of our neighborhood. As soon as the problem became evident early in the day, prisoners from the penitentiary, accompanied by a guard, were ordered to walk the entire length of the acequia system, starting on Acequia Madre Street (where the mother ditch began). After walking down several city streets, they eventually discovered the dammed area. In order to free up all the boards and rocks, one of the prisoners dove into the deep end of the pond. The others broke up the top of the dam with shovels, releasing a gush of water, and they watched as it slowly gathered momentum and

New Mexico State Penitentiary, Cerrillos Road. Photo courtesy Robert "Satch" Trujillo.

flowed in the direction of the penitentiary. It wasn't too long before the rain resumed and the boys began gathering and stacking river rocks to rebuild their dam, and swimming was on the next afternoon's schedule again. If it was late Friday or Saturday, the guards wouldn't bother to break up the dam over the weekend, but they arrived like clockwork on Monday morning, prisoners in tow. The boys were so fascinated with the demeanor, mannerisms, and tattoos of the prisoners that they would deliberately dam the culvert just so they could spend a few moments talking to them.

The State Penitentiary, a group of brick buildings several blocks long at the end of Cordova Road, was surrounded by high walls and barbed-wire fences and served as an unspoken reminder to us that crime didn't pay. A women's prison stood next door. and I couldn't imagine what crimes women could commit to warrant imprisoning them there. Dad said some women could be every bit as mean as a man, and sometimes meaner. "Don't kid yourself. Some women can lift a man over their heads and toss him twenty feet," he said as I listened, wide-eyed. Although I never met one of these Amazonian women, I kept my eye out for one any time I sat in the park downtown.

Armed with this information, we never wandered too close to the prison for fear of being grabbed by one of the prisoners, who in our imagination stood watching as we walked by. We also never knew when one of the inmates was going to escape, and although it had not happened, we always feared the possibility. As part of his newspaper route, my brother Jimmy recalls delivering copies of the local newspaper to the Pen in 1952. "One afternoon, I was getting my papers ready to deliver. After folding about fifty of them, I stacked them in my bag and secured them to the handlebars of the bike. All of a sudden we heard loud sirens blaring throughout the city. A bunch of us jumped on our bikes and headed in the direction of the Pen to see what happened, leaving our newspapers scattered on the porch. A roadblock was set up before we got there. The police told us to stay where we were. In a short while we found out that a group of prisoners were involved in a riot, and that some of them had been shot." Hearing the news, my mother locked the doors, drew back the curtains, and kept us in the house until the sirens stopped.

Adding to my already burgeoning fears, my sister Anita whispered that they had an electric chair in one of the small buildings and that every time our lights flickered, it meant that another prisoner had been fried to a crisp. Though it is hard to believe, we thought about it every time the house lights dimmed, even for a moment; we were gullible enough to believe this far-fetched rumor. There actually was an electric chair at the prison, but I'm not sure how often it was used or if the flickering of lights coincided with it.

During the summer, fishing could always occupy one's time. Dad loved to fish, and I was always a willing companion, even though it meant being attacked by mosquitoes and walking endless miles. Before we sat along the banks of the Pecos River, we first had to travel twenty-five miles east of Santa Fe, then another ten over rocky dirt roads and muddy ruts to reach Dad's favorite fishing spots, the first at Cow Creek, and another, favored later in the day, a few miles up the road at Bull Creek, where the trout put up a good fight. Sometimes we walked across a rickety bridge made from two thick metal cables at waist length, with wooden slats tied together with wire to form the walkway. The rushing river was only a foot or two beneath us, and less than twenty feet long, yet it seemed to me as though we were maneuvering the expanse of the Grand Canyon. I held on tightly to the cables on each side, fearful that I would fall in the river and be carried off by the current.

A few times during the summer, Cousin Ramona's new husband Amarante Chávez invited Dad to go fishing, and we knew it would be special. Monte had worked as the maître d' at the historic La Fonda Hotel in Santa Fe for a number of years, and through his long association with some of the guests, he received many perks. Occasionally he was invited to fish at the Greer Garson Fogelson Ranch in Pecos. In the early 1950s, the actress with the flaming red hair and her oilman husband, Buddy Fogelson, bought a large plot of land in Pecos that they named the Forked Lightning Ranch and remodeled the ranch house to suit their more urban needs. The original ranch had been a stage stop on the Old Santa Fe Trail and served as Union headquarters during the Civil War when battles were fought at nearby Glorieta Pass in 1862. For years, the Fogelsons spent summers at the ranch and visited Santa Fe often, dining at the La Fonda Hotel and attending local artistic and social functions.

Arriving at the ranch early one morning, Monte took us to the main house to check in and was greeted at the door by Greer Garson. He introduced my father, who was rendered speechless by her beauty, and she reached over and patted my head, laughing about the fact that we were both redheads. I mumbled something about not being Irish and felt my cheeks turn deep red.

The fishing holes on this property were the best on the Pecos River, and many were virtually unfished since the ranch was privately owned. As we followed the bank of the river, the ground cracked with delight, announcing our presence to the squirrels and chipmunks. It was as though we had been transported to paradise. I was awed by the splendor of the ranch, but Monte took it all in stride. The Santa Fe National Forest bordered the property, and it had four miles of private frontage on the Pecos River, with fishing holes considered the best in the area. The musky smell of piñon and juniper trees floated through the air, complemented by gentle breezes scattering the scent of the many willow trees around the main house, where bright yellow wasps buzzed endlessly under the low-hanging branches. There were no thirsty patches in the greenery that covered every square foot as far as the eye could see. Wildflowers dotted the grassy knolls forming rows of color.

Monte was a seasoned fisherman, and we headed immediately to his favorite spot where the fishing was exceptional, with hungry rainbow trout jumping out of the water anxious to snatch our bait. The excitement of trout fishing was tempered only by the food. This was no sack-lunch trip; no tortillas here. The chef at La Fonda prepared a special basket for Monte with such delicacies as tomatoes stuffed with tuna and crab, potato and macaroni salads, and buttery, flaky pastries, followed by a bottle of Chianti that he enjoyed at the end of the meal.

The dozen or two fish Monte and my dad caught made a great dinner for our family when we returned home. I never caught a fish, though; the water was always too fast. It whisked tree branches down the river with ease, along with my line, hooks, and worms. Actually, my preferred bait was bubble gum or chunks of corn, since I found touching a worm to be unappetizing, let alone piercing a hook through it. I spent most of my time untangling my line from the roots and rocks in the middle of the river.

Years later, when I finally hooked a fish, it caught me off guard as the fish pulled abruptly on my pole. In the excitement, I fell forward and ended up in the mud at the edge of the pond. In one swift move, Dad retrieved me, my pole, and the ten-inch fish, which Mother later cooked for dinner. These were stocked pond fish, for which we paid the property owner in Cienega five dollars to spend a few hours fishing and five cents an inch for the one we caught.

Dad and I also spent weekends walking through foothills and jagged trails around Santa Fe County, Geiger counter in hand, hoping to strike it rich. In the early 1950s, many times we headed up a narrow mountain road a few miles off the Albuquerque highway. The air was crisp and clean. Dad was driving his 1948 Ford pickup and whistling a tune. We were going prospecting for uranium...we were off to see the Wizard...and we were going to be rich! The truck sputtered up the winding dirt road. These were no ordinary roads, but two deep ruts in which the tires seemed to fit quite comfortably. There was no guardrail on the right, just a steep drop. In some places we barely had enough space to travel around the curves. As I looked up ahead, I wondered what would happen if we fell off the road. My mind wandered back to the landscape as I spotted a covey of quail walking single file, with the parents taking up the front and back. An occasional dragonfly flitted by my arm, followed by mosquitoes of various sizes. We parked the truck in the shade, a short distance from the road. We searched for outcroppings of rocks whose triangular edges protruded from the ground, hoping to find a field of uranium, a radioactive mineral for which Dad said the government paid lots of money. Dad said if we found an outcropping, we would have to file papers at the county courthouse to stake a claim. I had no idea of what type of rock this uranium resembled, and I'm not sure Dad did either, but we believed it was green in color, and I imagined that it would sound like the ticking of a clock gone berserk as the Geiger counter scanned over it and that the shriek of it would force me to cover my ears. Every so often an ordinary rock would emit a small amount of radioactivity, but never the sound we were hoping for. Uranium turned out to be elusive.

Each time we went prospecting, we brought back boxes full of "treasure rocks" in the back of the truck, but never uranium. There were geodes, ugly on the outside, but when you split them in half with a hammer, the insides sparkled like a bowl filled with diamonds. Small rock formations called fairy crosses scattered on the ground next to sheets of sparkling mica that peeled off like tissue paper. We brought home red rocks, green rocks, and blue rocks that we dragged into the bathroom, then closed the curtains and turned off the lights so we could scan them with a black light to see if they glowed the uranium green. They never did. Today, these treasures are buried somewhere deep in the backyard, to be unearthed a hundred years from now by archaeologists probing the old neighborhoods of Santa Fe.

Piñon nuts (pine nuts) were a delicacy we looked forward to at the end of most summers. These are raisin-sized, brown-shelled nuts that grow in a cone on the piñon tree, and have been a staple food for both Pueblo and Spanish people for centuries. The nuts fall from their cones and create a thick, brown, nutty blanket under the tree, which makes them fairly easy to harvest. In a cycle common to pine trees, there was a local crop every three to seven years around late September and October. Although family outings were rare, when piñon time came around, we all climbed into the backseat of the car or an uncle's truck and headed out. The cool breeze was invigorating as we headed toward Seton Village, one of the great piñon-picking locations, about a half-hour drive southeast of Santa Fe on the highway to Las Vegas. In addition to the piñon picking, it was also an opportunity for the adults to enjoy sharing a six-pack of beer in the late summer sun. As my sister Rosalie and I searched for just the right tree, Mom would spread a sheet under a large piñon tree, and one of the men would shake it, loosening the nuts from their dry cones. The fallen piñons would be gathered from the sheet and put into a flour sack or pillowcase, the debris to be removed later.

At the end of the picking, we spread out our lunch, baloney and cheese on a tortilla, followed by a large Mason jar of water. Later, we loaded our bags into the vehicle and headed back to Santa Fe as the pumpkin yellow sun began to set. Once home, we separated the pine needles and dirt from the piñons and washed them in a bucket and spread them out on a table to dry overnight. The next day, Mom placed a layer of piñon on a flat pan and baked them in the oven, checking them every five minutes or so until the insides were cooked. She usually gave us a handful as they came out of the oven but kept most of them hidden away to be enjoyed in the middle of winter and baked in Christmas treats. Every so often my sister and I sat at the kitchen table cracking cooked piñon with a rolling pin, enough to fill a shot glass for Dad's evening snack, which he would sprinkle with salt and eat by the handful.

Shelling each seed was a tedious process, so various methods were attempted, one of which included using a rolling pin. We

placed a layer of unshelled piñon on the table, and then with just
the right amount of pressure, we rolled a rolling pin over the
entire amount. This resulted in most of the shells cracking so
they could be easily separated. Too much pressure resulted in
piñon mush; not enough pressure was useless. The best method
for cracking piñon was cracking them with your teeth, one by
one, and spitting out the shell. No rocket science here.

The neighborhood boys couldn't wait for piñon-picking season to begin. From the cuartito next to their house, Cousin
Junior retrieved a few gunnysacks. The boys rode their bikes
down Camino del Monte Sol toward Sun Mount, gathered up
pine cones by hand from select trees, and returned home hours
later with several sacks full. They'd spend the next few hours
roasting the *piñas* on a screen placed over a fire built in a hole
that was bordered by river rocks until the cones opened. Then
they removed the nuts with their fingernails as the pine cone
cooled. This was a messy process, and the sticky pine pitch,
trementina, stayed on their hands and had to be removed with
gobs of lard. There is no way to describe the delicious, heady
aroma emanating from the roasting pine cones that drifted in
the air over the neighborhood. It was a smell like no other, recognizable even by small children.

Many families picked piñon nuts as a cottage industry.
Parents and kids camped out for weeks at a time, gathering hundreds of pounds of piñon that they would sell to individuals and
stores around town, who would in turn resell them at a price
more than double what they paid. Occasionally the newspaper
would run a story about a comment made by a tourist driving by
these areas pertaining to how religious these people from Santa
Fe were as they knelt praying by the trees next to the road. They
would have been surprised to learn we were harvesting nuts.

We were warned that eating too many piñons could result in
a variety of maladies. Any ailment involving the throat was sure
to be blamed on too much piñon, as well as the occasional
unsightly and painful boils that erupted on the skin of our
behinds, which made it difficult to sit down. Both were quickly
forgotten by the next season. I recently read somewhere that
today it takes more than a million pounds of piñon to satisfy the

demands of the Southwest. In those days, we were pretty happy with the ten or fifteen pounds we gathered.

The boys in our neighborhood traveled in a much wider circle than the girls. My brothers and their friends covered distances that included all areas of the city, Fort Marcy, Canyon Road, and Agua Fria. In later years, they rode on bicycles to Hyde Park, the ski basin, and Arroyo Hondo, more than ten miles in each direction. But in my mind, Santa Fe was only about two miles in diameter. The farthest I ever strayed from home was on warm summer days when we walked from our house to the top of Sun Mount, Monte Sol, east of the old Santa Fe Trail and the street named for the mountain, Camino del Monte Sol. What a feat— to us it was comparable to climbing Mount Everest. We arose early in the morning, gathered our tortilla sandwiches and a jar of water, and then rounded up the neighborhood kids who were going along. Most of the time there were about five of us. This serious expedition covered an area of about five miles due east from our house to the top of the mountain. We climbed slowly, stopping often to catch our breath. The mountain added about a thousand feet to the city's seven thousand foot elevation. When we reached the summit, we lingered for a while, sitting on the flat ground to eat lunch, while looking out at the splendor of the city below. We often encountered other groups who were relaxing in the shade under the trees. Coming down the mountain evoked giggles as we repeatedly lost our footing on the fast slide down. We arrived home hot, sore, and exhausted.

Cousin Gilbert occasionally invited us to swim at the Carlos Viera house at the corner of East Coronado and Old Santa Fe Trail. It was the only house for miles around that area and one of the largest in Santa Fe. This was a huge, multiroomed house with foot-thick adobe walls, vigas, and south-facing portals. A large swimming pool sat on one side of the immense yard. Through Uncle Joe, who had worked for the new owners as caretaker for many years after Viera's death in 1937, neighborhood kids were allowed to swim in the pool right before it was scheduled to be drained and cleaned. Viera was a famous artist, one of the first of the Santa Fe painters in the 1920s. He was also one of few people in Santa Fe who piloted his own plane, which he flew to Indian pueblos around Santa Fe.

The thought of swimming in a real private pool was cause for excitement. Unlike the municipal pool, which had opened recently and accommodated as many screaming kids as could squeeze into an eight-by-thirty-foot area, we would have this luxury all to ourselves. I was about ten years old and had never been swimming, but I knew it involved some sort of arm and leg movement. I believed it was a natural process, like walking, although I had never had an opportunity to test my theory. I was not quite four feet tall, and I jumped with abandon into the five-foot deep end and immediately sank as though weighted down by a lead cannonball. I felt myself being carried by spirals of water, which wound themselves around me. I recall rising to the surface and sinking again, my eyes focusing to see multicolored ribbons of light that cascaded through the warm water. Going down for the third time, I heard my cousin Gilbert hollering in the distance as I struggled to awaken from what seemed to be a trancelike, peaceful state, where time had all but stopped. He demanded to know what the hell I was doing and didn't I know how to swim, and then he yanked me out of the water, coughing and sputtering. He made me sit at the side of the pool for the rest of the afternoon. With that experience, the desire to be near water left me. The fear of drowning has lived deep inside me since that incident. These days, I still get woozy standing on the shore of a small pond, and oceans completely overwhelm me.

Chapter Twelve

NEIGHBORHOOD BULLIES
AND OTHER OBSTACLES

Life in the neighborhood wasn't always peaceful, particularly if you had to contend with the neighborhood bully. She didn't like anybody and strutted around the neighborhood, intimidating small kids and dogs. My brothers called her the "What-choo-lookee." Any time you looked her way, she would holler, "What choo looking at?" and come running after you. No matter how hard you tried, you were never going to get close to her, unless she decided to hit you. I guess I was always on her bad side, although I was never certain she had a good side. She was even-tempered: always mad, always mean. And she was built, as the boys would say, like a brick shithouse, strong and muscular, and with a nasty disposition to boot.

Walking to school was enough of a burden, but having her lurk behind you or ahead of you was worse. If she was ahead, she waited until you caught up; and if you crossed the street, so did she. If she was behind, no matter how your pace quickened, she was always right at your heels. And to make it worse, there were certain places on the route to school where you needed to stay on the right side of the street, because life presented obstacles when you least expected them. Near the center of Galisteo Street, right before we turned onto the street leading to elementary school, lived a short little man who most mornings would stand next to the wall, waiting for someone to come by. He would terrorize anyone walking on the left side of the street. He was about four and a half feet tall, and he mumbled and yelled and generally scared the bejesus out of everyone under sixteen (except our neighborhood bully, who wasn't easily intimidated and walked right past him). So if the bully didn't get you, he would (although I'm not sure he ever "got" anyone, and we weren't willing to find out).

Always in your face, the bully carried on with nonstop threats of "Wanna fight? Wanna fight? What's the matter, choo scared?" I was usually relieved to see the cafeteria building in front of Wood-Gormley Elementary School off in the near distance, since I knew I wouldn't have to deal with her again until three o'clock. And if I was lucky, I would dash out of school, using every shortcut I knew to get home without running into her again.

But summer was a different story. She had more time to terrorize, and like most bullies, she picked on people smaller than herself. Once after a long period of harassment, or for some other unknown reason (maybe I had Wheaties for breakfast that morning), I agreed to fight her in "the field," a vacant lot just south of our neighborhood where we played baseball and waded up to our waists after a heavy summer rainstorm. The momentum built up for several days...the neighborhood buzzed with excitement, or at least I thought it did...I walked with my back straight, chest forward, knowing that I would emerge victorious...the What-choo-lookee would never make my life miserable again. Minutes turned to hours, hours into days, days into nights...and then the day arrived.

There was no getting out of it, and shortly after noon I walked bravely down the street, Within moments we were standing face to face in the middle of a crowd of prodding spectators (at least it looked like a crowd—well, a bunch of kids, anyway). I knew then how David felt facing Goliath. I also knew I was not destined to be a fighter; not only was I not strong enough, tall enough, or brave enough, but I knew I was, in fact, a sacrificial lamb. I was about to be laid out on a mud altar and left to die. I was going to be pounded and pummeled. I was going to go through life without any teeth. As the tension built, I envisioned myself lying in a bed at St. Vincent's Hospital, a plaster cast from head to toe, every visible surface autographed by family and friends, two black eyes peeking out from the bandages on my face.

As she roared her menacing "Come onnnnnnnnnnnn," I braced myself for the blows she was surely going to inflict. I stepped back quickly and felt the breeze from her swinging punch. Maybe I could dance away from her flesh-pounding blows. I became quick, agile, moving like a whirling dervish, dodging every movement. She was a regular Sugar Ray Robinson. I was so engrossed in my quest to outsmart, outmove, outdance, and out-maneuver, I didn't notice the huge puddle of muddy water behind me. One big shove and I was up to my red head in mud. Like a lightning bolt she was on top of me as my pearl-rimmed eye-glasses flew off. She was far stronger than I ever imagined, and I knew I didn't have a chance. Pushing and shoving matches with my siblings hadn't prepared me for this. I was doomed.

Just then the rescue squad arrived. My brother Jimmy grabbed her off me with one hand, picked me up out of the pud-dle of water with the other, and told us to get the hell out of there and if he ever caught her looking at me sideways, he would kick her ass until her teeth rattled. Her glare could have burned a hole through stone, and she was ready to take him on, but she must have had second thoughts since she was silent behind me as we trudged up the hill going to our respective houses. I was grateful she didn't decide to finish the job then. From that day on, she mostly ignored me, and we never exchanged words, not even bad ones. In recent years I have seen her at the grocery store, in church, or walking down the street, but she always turns her gaze away.

Other childhood perils also existed. Occasionally we were exposed to dirty old men, or rather, they were exposed to us. My mother referred to these men as *sin vergüenza*, scoundrels without an ounce of shame. By unspoken agreement, these people were never discussed at the dinner table. One such person, a man in his thirties who lived in one of the outlying neighborhoods, apparently got his thrills by spying on children, little girls in particular.

At the age of seven, I wouldn't have known what a dirty old man was. Typically, my cousins and I played in the sand pile in my backyard, right under the clothesline, where a rickety, barbed-wire–like fence took over where the pumice block wall ended. Every so often a voice would urge us in a whisper, "Hey little girls, come here. I have something for you."

Curiously drawn to this mysterious invitation, once we walked over to the window of the old shed, and since part of the building was a few feet beneath the surface, the windows were close to the ground. As we approached the screen, we spotted a man's outline. We didn't realize he was naked until we stepped up to the window, screamed in unison, and made a speedy 180-degree turn and raced the fifty feet home. This man regularly exposed himself to innocent young girls as though it was as natural as breathing. Any time he would meander across the yard into that small storeroom, we knew what was going to happen, and we ran in the opposite direction. My oldest sister Anita occasionally crossed into that yard to return sugar or eggs to Prima Kika, the neighbor across the wall. Since several houses made up that compound, he would sometimes be watering the plants and trees as a handyman. On one occasion, he grabbed my sister by the arm and offered her a dime. She didn't wait around to see what the dime was for and instead pulled away and dashed home.

We hardly ever played in the sand pile when he was nearby, and I always wondered why another adult didn't grab him by the genitals and put a stop to his behavior. Everyone simply accepted that he was "different," and we were warned to stay away from the shed and never look into the windows again. It was as though a silent conspiracy existed to protect the guilty. They seemed to think if they ignored the problem, it would eventually go away.

This behavior apparently wasn't limited to just neighbors. A bone doctor, an osteopath with an office in a nearby neighborhood, preyed on innocent victims in a more subtle manner. On one occasion, I fell off my bicycle and began to suffer severe head and neck pain, so I was taken to see him. As I sat in the reception room, my name was called, but my mother was instructed to remain behind "to arrange for payment." In the examination room, I was told to disrobe completely and cover myself with the sheet. As I lay quietly on the table anticipating some sort of chiropractic manipulation (perhaps an instantaneous cure), the doctor began to push his genitals against my toes while clutching my ankles. No nurse was present in the room, and I was too naïve to realize that this wasn't part of the treatment. It didn't occur to me until years later that this man was a child molester. He treated a number of patients, primarily women and children, and eventually expanded his practice and moved to another neighborhood. At the time, I thought it pointless to mention the bizarre treatment; after all, he *was* the *doctor*, and children did not question adults. Fortunately my headaches subsided, and I never had occasion to return to his office.

Chapter Thirteen

CHILDHOOD ILLNESS AND HOME REMEDIES

Mostly because of our family's lack of money, only a serious illness or injury warranted a visit to a doctor, and then we would be taken to Dr. Gonzales's office, where, depending on the time of arrival, the wait could last as long as five hours. He was a general practitioner who treated everything from the common cold to warts. IIis sccrctary extensively quizzed everyone who called for an appointment about his or her symptoms. Then they would have to repeat it all over again when they finally saw the doctor. Due to her information gathering, it wouldn't be unusual for a person walking down the street to be asked how his or her visit with the doctor went, having gotten the information from the secretary in one way or another.

Although I'm not sure her inquisitiveness was intentional, the gossipy secretary annoyed my dad to such an extent that he would calmly tell her nothing was wrong and he just wanted to see the doctor, to which she replied that she needed to know the reason for this visit first. Since conversations were held in the waiting room for all to hear, there were no secrets, and everyone's ears perked up when she asked questions. On one visit, Dad finally lost his patience and loudly declared, "I'm having labor pains. I think the baby's coming." The shocked secretary was both speechless and embarrassed, mumbled something, and motioned him to sit down. Although she continued her practice with other patients, she never asked him for information again, each time ushering him into the examination room in haughty silence.

It was a long walk from home to the doctor's office downtown, but when a worrisome illness made it necessary, Mom would bundle us up and we'd take off. Since the men were at work and most of the women didn't drive, there were few rides, and our little hearts pumped feverishly as we dragged ourselves forward, confident relief would be forthcoming. After the long wait to see the doctor, we then walked to the pharmacy for a prescription, and then home. Fortunately, most of the time we were treated at home.

I developed several ploys to stay home from school, my favorite of which was to warm a washcloth on the gas heater in our bedroom and place it on my forehead. When Mom would come in to wake us up for school, I would ask her to check if I had a fever. Concerned mother that she was, she dutifully tested my forehead, and if it was warm enough, decided I should stay home. I'm not sure my sister Rosalie bought this story, because I would be the recipient of *the glance* before she left for school. A few times this ploy didn't work, so sometimes I also wasted a whole night's sleep with my feet hanging out from the covers hoping I would catch a cold.

Sometimes one of us was seriously ill, and that's when Mom started peeling potatoes. Any moment, you would feel the relief brought on by cool potatoes placed on your forehead. Thin slices soaked in vinegar were lined in a row, followed by a vinegar-soaked cotton strip to cover them, tied at the back of the head. The potatoes were supposed to soak up the fever. Whether or not the theory had any scientific basis, it never failed to provide relief, real or imagined. It might have been just the tender loving care that accompanied the process, but we always felt better. Remedies made from osha, an aromatic root, were popular for soothing a sore throat, colds, and congestion. We also had other remedies: putting saliva and salt on an ant bite; or applying crushed rose petals to mouth sores or sore throats. Not only did the petals have a pleasing taste, but they seemed to soothe the inflammation. The petals had been dried in the sun, sprinkled with sugar, toasted in the oven, and finally placed in a storage jar. Tying a couple of garlic buds on a string and wearing it around your neck was the worst remedy. This would ward off not only vampires, but also the common cold.

I never knew what my mother meant when she said *"te vas a empachar"* when we ate raw cookie dough or bread dough that hadn't cooled down, or when we swallowed a wad of bubble gum, a habit we were all guilty of. The word defied translation, but I had the distinct impression she was referring to a stomachache, and the way the adults carried on, you'd have thought it was fatal. Apparently it could be. The term referred to a blockage in the stomach, where the intestines stuck together and kept food from traveling through the final digestive stage. If you complained of the right symptoms, it was necessary to massage the abdomen to alleviate the condition. If that didn't work, a *sobadora* (masseuse) or *curandera* (healer) would have to be called to professionally massage or prescribe herbs. In the worst of circumstances, a visit to Dr. Gonzales would be in order. In the meantime, a hot cup of yerba buena, home-grown peppermint tea, followed the massage. In place of a heating pad, Mom warmed a dinner plate on the stove or in the oven, wrapped it in a light towel, and placed it on the affected area. When it cooled to the touch, she replaced it with another warmed plate. This method was also effective for sore muscles when accompanied by *ventosas.* A small votive candle placed on the afflicted area of the body was carefully lit and a small drinking glass placed over it. The candle immediately extinguished to create suction, allowing the glass to be slowly moved in circles to massage the area. This was repeated several times until relief came. The circular impressions of the glass remained on the skin until the next day.

Art Romero (Dad's cousin) at Art's Drug Store, 1950s. Photo courtesy Amelia Hollis Romero.

We were repeatedly cautioned not to sit or sleep near open windows, or we would be afflicted with *aigre*, a headache caused by a draft or breeze, particularly if your neck was sweaty. For this reason, Dad never liked to ride in a car with the windows opened, not even on the hottest of days. Every time I snuck the windows open a crack, he complained of a headache.

For various ailments, other remedies could be purchased at Art's Drug Store, which was next to the El Fidel Hotel. Lydia Pinkham's Vegetable Compound was prescribed for the relief of menstrual cramps. This bitter tasting brown liquid was twenty percent alcohol and advertised in magazines and newspapers as "good for what ails you." I imagine the alcohol content might have contributed to the "feeling better sensation" some patients experienced from taking it.

Rosebud Salve, a pink aromatic salve in a small, royal blue tin decorated with red roses, was widely used to treat most all skin ailments, from burns to rashes. Primarily sold door-to-door by budding entrepreneurs, every medicine cabinet in Santa Fe had it. Anyone who filled out an order form would receive a box with five to ten tins of the salve. Sold for fifty cents each, the money was carefully wrapped in paper and sent to the company in the envelope provided, accompanied by a form requesting the premium chosen from the catalog. Most kids in our neighborhood tried their hand at selling, but a lot of salve had to be sold to qualify for the better premiums, those that moved beyond the plastic or rubber trifle. Interest in selling the product and its white counterpart in a larger tin usually diminished after parents ended up with a medicine cabinet full of these cans. A recent trip to the health food store surprisingly produced two small tins of this treasured salve with its unmistakable rosy smell, still a perfect remedy for the chapped lips caused by wintry weather.

Chapter Fourteen

KEEPING THE CUPBOARDS FULL

Most residential sections of Santa Fe had a *tiendita*, usually a home in which one or two rooms were converted to a store and where you could buy almost all of the staples necessary to a household. On weekends, adults stopped by these stores to purchase flour, sugar, and meat, and engaged in the latest mitote.

Children loved the neighborhood store. Every extra penny we begged or pilfered from our parents bought our favorite Bazooka Bubble Gum, with which, if the advertising was true, you could blow a bubble so big that you might even fly away. *Who knew?* On the metal shelves within reach of small hands were PayDays, Dots, and other popular candy bars. Refrigerated cases housed Popsicles of every color and small cups of vanilla ice cream. For many of us not accustomed to such sweetness, our favorite treat was a banana cream pie–flavored turnover, a delicious yellow cake folded over just like an empanadita, our traditional homemade fruit turnover, and filled to overflowing with a mouth-watering, creamy white filling.

The little store in our neighborhood, about five doors from our house, was run by Dad's cousin, Manuel Romero, and his wife Ruby. They purchased the store in the mid-1940s from the original developer of the neighborhood, Don Canuto Romero, who sold mostly candy and other trifles. Here we were allowed to charge items to the family account. Once Uncle Joe came in to complain about a large monthly statement and discovered that Cousin Ramona was charging large amounts of candy each day after school. He put a quick stop to that practice, forbidding her to go anywhere near the store.

Another tiendita we frequented was on Galisteo Street, near Berger Street, and run by the Herburgers. We stopped there every day after school for a fire-hot cinnamon sucker, a succulent, tongue-teasing, red candy square on a stick. Frank Ortíz owned yet another store further up Galisteo Street at its intersection with Hickox Street. He stocked a wide variety of groceries and probably had more customers than the other two combined. He was one of the first to sell beer and liquor, commodities the older boys in the neighborhood lusted after.

Every few months, Jimmy and his gavilla hung out under the bridge next to the store and waited patiently for the last light in the building to flicker out, sometimes as late as midnight. A half hour or so later, they crept to the back of the store, where one of the boys would break a window, climb into the store, and let the others in.

"Hurry up," Jimmy admonished as the last one walked through the door.

"Get down! There's a damn car coming," someone said as they all hit the floor.

"Oh, shit! I dropped the damn flashlight, wait a minute...OK," someone said as he reached for a six-pack of Acme beer.

"Hey," one of them whispered. "I'm getting a couple of these bottles of La Boheme. We can sell it to the winos!"

"OK, but let's get the hell out of here," urged Jimmy.

They gathered up as much beer and liquor as they could carry and hightailed it back to our neighborhood. Then they'd spend the next few hours sitting in Emilio's broken-down 1936 Chevy parked in the vacant lot at the end of our street next to Uncle Rumaldo's house. This beat-up, old green car served as the official clubhouse where they chug-a-lugged beer, and they would barely be able to get up for school the next day. They never stole groceries or money but returned periodically to replenish their stock of beer, especially on hot summer nights. Every so often, Mr. Ortíz would return to the store after closing, never noticing the boys lying flat between the aisles, shaking in their shoes.

Eventually larger grocery stores replaced the neighborhood stores. Bat-Rite, Safeway, and Piggly Wiggly stores popped up in various locations throughout the city. The nearest Piggly Wiggly was two blocks away on Cordova Road, where a small shopping center began to take root and included DeCastro Jewelers, where Dad would occasionally buy Mother gifts and pay for them over time. Piggly Wiggly gave out S&H Green Stamps as shopping premiums, and in our neighborhood the kitchen drawers were filled to capacity with perforated sheets of stamps waiting for someone to begin the unsavory task of licking and pasting them to the pages of a small, green book. Filled books were set aside until enough were collected for the desired premium. In our family, since grocery shopping was sometimes not even a weekly event, stamps were hard to come by. Luckily, we had school friends who worked at Piggly Wiggly, and they not only charged us less for groceries, but loaded us down with as many stamps as they could stuff in the bag. Wednesdays were double stamp days, and many of the housewives waited until then to do their shopping, but we had double and triple stamp days almost every time we went shopping.

The S&H redemption catalog was one of the most popular, more so than the Gold Bond stamps catalog offered by other stores. Two books could be exchanged for something as minimal as a plastic lunch pail, plastic bowls, or a plastic toy. More books could be redeemed for towels, sheets, blankets, toasters, mixers, and other kitchen appliances and household decorations.

We saved our nickels and dimes for specialty stores where we could buy bountiful scoops of homemade ice cream. Coming from the high school downtown, many teens wandered into the soda shop on Burro Alley next to the Lensic Theater. Many times we stopped at Free Fraser Pharmacy, at the corner of College and Manhattan Streets, where we sat at the soda fountain and sometimes ordered a lime or cherry phosphate instead of Coca-Cola. The rest of the time, under the watchful eyes of the clerks, we spent browsing through the counters full of perfumes and cosmetics, magazines we would never read, and the expensive boxes of name-brand chocolates we would never taste. The saleslady's gaze followed our every move, as though we were not worthy of thinking about the merchandise, let alone touching it, and surely not buying it.

During recess, lunchtime, and after school during elementary and junior high school days, we spent time at Della's Place. Della Collyer was a tall, orange-haired, fiftyish woman and was very white, her cheeks abundantly powdered with very red rouge. She ran the little concession store located in the alley behind Wood-Gormley School, said "damn" a lot, and lived a few blocks away in a large brick house on Galisteo Street. A kid fortunate enough to possess that wondrous commodity, lunch money, could shop to his or her heart's content for goodies not found in the neighborhood store: every kind and color of bubble gum balls and jelly beans, hot dogs, potato chips, and Cokes. With our meager budget, our fare was mostly the penny stuff, and we took our time making a selection. Della's store was open all through our elementary and junior high years. It was a green, ramshackle wood shack, but it was warm inside. She knew everyone by name and had a list of students' names and addresses furnished by the school secretary, just in case anyone ever decided to help themselves without paying. She treated most of the Spanish kids with disdain, watching them closely until they left on their own or by shooing them out the door. She never gave out any free samples. She made sure shoplifting was impossible, not only by watching every move you made, but by placing the more expensive food items out of the reach of small hands. She ran her business well into the 1960s, with the place becoming more dilapidated with each passing year.

Chapter Fifteen

Teen Years, Dating, and Other Hazards

It felt like we grew up gradually and quietly, maturing at a slower pace than our Anglo counterparts. Sometimes in junior high but more often in high school, teen pregnancies popped up as if from nowhere. These were confusing times because some of us couldn't even get a date, and the ones voted most likely to succeed were getting pregnant and being thrown into family life. Though small in number, there were still more pregnant Spanish girls than Anglos; or at least, Anglo pregnancies were better-kept secrets. You can bet it all happened at the Yucca Drive-In Theater in the backseat of a '56 Pontiac or Chevy.

Young girls barely out of puberty turned up pregnant. They came from both influential, upper middle-class families and the families of the rest of us. Wealthy parents shipped their pregnant daughters "out of the country" or to "modeling school" during their senior years, and the alleged pregnancies were never discussed upon their return. On the other side of the coin, girls from poorer families went on to give birth and immediately gave them up for adoption or left them to be raised by their mothers, women who wore the title of Grandmother far too early in their lives.

Pregnant teens wore baggy clothes and heavy coats, even on warm days, shrugging off the change in body size and blaming the expanding waist on too many burgers and milkshakes. Even in our naïveté, we knew those extra pounds were really a baby, but couldn't imagine ourselves being in that predicament. Personally, I was too immature to comprehend what these girls were going through, but I knew that if it happened to anyone in our neighborhood, our parents would have disowned us. Yet some girls wore the pregnancy like a banner. While some girls rode off into the sunset never to be heard from again, some came back to finish school and face the snickers and whispers. It seemed to me that though they had survived the ordeal, the sparkle in their eyes was dimmed.

As a group, we knew nothing about birth control. Whispered rumors abounded about sex, who was doing it and how it was done, and birth control methods ranging from insertion of a well-shaken bottle of Coke to bathing in Clorox, as well as other kinds of bizarre methods to purge one's guilt. Rumor had it that only the guys were enjoying sex at the expense of many a young girl's virtue. Whispered endearments—"Will you still respect me after?"; "Sure, baby. You know I love you"; "*Tú nomás*, honey."—turned seemingly innocent encounters into short-lived moments of passion. Probably more than half of the hastily planned weddings every summer were accompanied by a shotgun, real or imagined. For the young and inexperienced, setting up housekeeping turned out to be more a nightmare than the American Dream. The girls next door became the wives of the class presidents and the football heroes. They discovered instant unhappiness instead of instant bliss. A seventeen-year-old in our group married his girlfriend of only a few months when she became pregnant. Three years later, two more children added great distress to teens barely able to feed themselves, let alone a family. They divorced shortly after the birth of their third child. But not everybody got burned—some of these impromptu marriages actually lasted more than a few years, some even seeing their twenty-fifth and fiftieth anniversaries.

Anglo teens appeared more worldly, and it seemed they discovered boys far earlier than the rest of us who agonized over the fact that we were not pretty enough or not shapely enough. But we didn't know that sometimes "putting out" equated with popularity. Despite my lack of popularity, since grade school I, too, always noticed when an exceptionally handsome Greek god enrolled in school, but I also knew I never had a chance once the popular girls moved in on him. Still, I wondered if he was aware of the impact he had on every young girl within a five-mile radius.

By the time my turn at high school came around in 1957, I noticed there were many couples. Most everyone hung out at Ingram's Drive-In, the teen "in" spot on Cerrillos Road, where hamburgers, fries, and Cokes were carried out on trays efficiently attached to the driver's side window by mostly young, pretty carhops. Teens sat in cars talking and laughing, listening to jukebox music blaring from the speakers.

The "Stompers," a group of teens whose name derived from square dancing and country music, congregated on one side of the parking lot next to their trucks, wearing crisply ironed cowboy shirts, Levis with ironed seams, boots, and cowboy hats. With few exceptions, that crowd was Anglo. A number of them were wannabee cowboys who had never sat on a horse, let alone ridden one. They rode around town in pickup trucks and smoked unfiltered cigarettes. The girls at their sides wore tight Levis and short-sleeved western shirts, their hair in ponytails. The demeanor of the Stompers was different from most teens. They were sometimes loud, brash, and arrogant, and they made no bones about not liking "all you greasers," a reference to anyone from our neighborhood. A number of them were rough and tough, hard smoking, and hard drinking, and they sat in class sneering, long legs stretched out into the aisle, daring anyone to ask them to move. When a girl quit her allegiance to the Stompers, she could be threatened and intimidated for going over to the "other side." The term *stomper*, as I understood it, meant someone who wore cowboy boots for not only kicking ass but for country-and-western dancing. These were not rock and rollers.

Then we had the Pachucos, a term taken from gangs in California that emerged in the forties. Some from that generation say there were few "real" Pachucos in Santa Fe, but many young Spanish teens began to emulate them in the early 1950s. The gangs hailed mostly from the barrios, neighborhoods on the west side of Santa Fe. There were the Westsiders, the Korchos (who hung out primarily on College Street), and the Lucianitos, and some who lived on Banana Hill, an area just off upper Alameda Street, among others. Dressed in baggy, tapered pants, they wore white T-shirts with rolled sleeves that held a pack of cigarettes. Chains hung from their belt loops into their pants pockets. They all sported tattoos including small crosses or dots on their right hand between the thumb and finger. These tattoos were made by pricking small holes in the skin with a needle or pin and wiping India ink over the area. The Pachucos spoke mostly Spanish and strutted with a recognizable arrogance. They spoke a jargon that set them apart from other teenagers, referring to each other as *"ese,"* or *"esa,"* and used *"chale"* for "no" and *"orale"* for "hello," along with a large vocabulary of words foreign to the average person.

My brother Bobby was one of these Pachucos, and he wore the title proudly. They had a certain gait, each step a slow and deliberate shuffle, hands in pockets. I watched with fascination as Bobby nailed a horseshoe-shaped metal tap onto the heel of his shoe and several smaller ones to the front sole. You could hear his footsteps clearly as he walked on the concrete sidewalk next to our driveway, and he annoyed my father as he walked through the house. They were renegades. The boys' side hair was slicked back with pomade, and the top hair was styled into a curly pouf. Bobby used to think he looked a little bit like Elvis Presley as he ran his fingers through his hair. (The girls wore their long hair in a high pompadour, the center of which it was rumored could easily conceal a switchblade knife.) Many of these young men had nicknames: Booza, Lechuga, Flattop, Gorilla, Flaco, Seco, Killer, Chango. But their families still referred to them by their given names. The Pachucos rarely hung out at the drive-ins with other teenagers, preferring to spend their time around the plaza.

On Friday nights everyone else headed to the Yucca Drive-In Theater at the outskirts of town. In the daytime, it was just a huge parking lot, with parking mounds at ten foot intervals and metal posts holding the speakers to hook on to the driver's side window. At night the lot was lit up like a Christmas tree, with a huge neon yucca plant on the back of the screen that faced Cerrillos Road. Heading toward the entrance, the driver paid admission for himself, and the three or four teens in the trunk struggled to keep from giggling as they pushed someone's foot or butt out of his or her face. Whispered death threats abounded after a gassy fart filled the air of the trunk. A well-placed piece of dark carpeting or several winter jackets could cover the person hiding on the floor of the backseat. Ticket sellers never came out of the booth to check, and if they knew, they turned a blind eye to the subterfuge. After parking in the last row, where there were not many overhead lights, the cramped trunk was emptied and the car driven closer to the concession stand. We feasted on hot dogs slathered with mustard and hot, buttered popcorn followed by icy Cokes, food we never ate at home.

At seventeen, I still had difficulty getting out at night. Dad became stricter as each year passed, at least with my sister Rosalie and me. As the oldest child, Anita had set a number of precedents for the rest of us. There was a twelve-year difference in our ages, so long before I became a teenager, she had already left home. Anita recalls that by the time she and her friends were thirteen, they were incurably boy-crazy. The students from St. Michael's Boys School were always in their midst, buying them sodas and milkshakes at Capitol Drug Store. "I remember Dad never let me go anywhere at night or on weekends. I would beg and cry for all I was worth, but he wasn't going to give in. It was really frustrating." After these sessions, she'd storm into the living room, slamming the door behind her. As soon as she

Prom Night, 1958,
Marie, Dad, Rosalie.

was sure Dad was asleep, she'd escape out the window like a flash. One of us always had to get up later that night to let her back in. Mother would sneak quietly out of bed and open the door for her, fearing Dad's wrath if he ever caught on.

Therefore, for prom night in 1958, both my sister and I dressed for the occasion. She and her boyfriend Jim were attending the dance, but I was just using it as an excuse to get out of the house. My dad begrudgingly stood with us in front of the fireplace in the living room for a picture. Had he known I wasn't going to the prom, there surely would have been hell to pay.

On other occasions Dad allowed me tag along with my sister and her boyfriend to a movie, but once out the door I'd meet up with my friend Rosalena. About eight of us hung out together, Ray Gene, Barry, Richard, Rudy, Mouse, Quack, Rosalena, and me. Since Rosalena's brother Ray Gene was part of that group, he had to include her, and I came along since I was her friend. Ray Gene, Richard, and Rudy were dating girls who were best friends, Ann, Glenna, and Nedra. The girls were Anglo, and in our minds the rest of us were "spicks," "beaners," "greasers," a fact we tried to ignore. Although we were rarely invited to the homes of these Anglo girls, occasionally when their parents were away, the whole group entered one of their houses for just a few minutes, but we were fearful of getting the girls into trouble.

These girls' houses were so different. Anglos lived in the newer residential districts of Santa Fe, away from the center of town where we usually hung out. Each family member had his or her own room, something difficult for us to imagine, and they had more than one bathroom, all indoors. The walls were decorated with floral paintings and family portraits, and there was modern furniture in the living room, which was used for living, not sleeping. Soft carpeting covered the floors and pleated curtains draped to the floor. The kitchen appliances gleamed, reflecting on the freshly waxed linoleum floor. There was no visible clutter; everything was in its place. Our house had two and a half rooms for seven children and one for our parents. Anglo families ate salad, steak, and baked potatoes on matched dinnerware. We ate beans and chile in bowls chipped from years of use. They ate bread; we ate tortillas. They wore different outfits each day; we wore the same homemade clothing three times a week. They ate at the school cafeteria; we carried our tortilla sandwich in a brown paper bag. They drove to school; we walked.

And these weren't the only differences. It seemed as though both Anglo and Spanish boys treated these "gringas" like goddesses and catered to their every whim, piling on charm obviously reserved for people they considered special. Their Anglo families treated them like princesses whose smiles lit up a room—and made us Spanish kids feel inadequate in their presence. They participated gladly in all the gym classes, wearing stark white tennis shoes with socks neatly folded over and bright red gym shorts, but we didn't. Our parents couldn't afford more clothes, especially gym uniforms, which were worn only once a week and then discarded at semester's end. (Although I was chosen by the faculty to be part of the cheerleading squad at Harrington Junior High in the seventh grade, my mother had to sew the red corduroy skirt lined with white satin. Along with the brown and white oxford shoes, sweater, and socks, it was an unexpected expense. Fortunately, each squad was chosen for only one year.) We had a dozen excuses why we couldn't play volleyball, whether it was a headache, stomach upset, or cramps. The P.E. teacher at Harrington was Mrs. York, a petite but muscular woman who wore gym shorts with sleeveless shirts, which showed off her physique. Every so often she tired of our excuses and ordered us out on the gym floor to participate in a game against the more experienced students, wearing our regular school clothes. I realized early on that I didn't know how to play volleyball and stood around pretending to pursue the ball, hoping the game would be over soon. It was as true in gym class as it was in every other activity: you were expected to already know the rules and how to play the game, but some of us, including me, didn't know a volleyball from a basketball. Even as a cheer- leader, I didn't know a fumble from a touchdown.

During the first semester of my sophomore year at Santa Fe High School, I had a classmate whose father owned an auto deal- ership in Santa Fe. We became friends and began to spend time together after school, probably more for her entertainment than mine. She was the richest person I'd ever known, and her wardrobe was the envy of every girl in school: fuzzy angora sweaters, felt skirts, silk scarves in every color, and penny loafers without even a tiny scuff. She drove a different car to school every week with a reckless, careless, don't-give-a-damn attitude. The glove compartment overflowed with traffic tickets crushed into pink wads resembling paper carnations. On any given afternoon, we walked to the five-and-dime after school, and, much to my surprise, she shoplifted everything in sight.

With my Catholic upbringing, simply being with her petri- fied me and I usually loitered around the other end of the store to wait until she headed for the exit. In my terror, I imagined the manager of the store placing us in handcuffs and the police descending on us. We would stand accused before a black-robed judge as my parents huddled in the background, Dad holding his hat in his hands, Mother dabbing her eyes, their heads hung in shame. As fate would have it, we got caught after a few times. I was at one end of the store thumbing through the teen magazines. Through the corner of my eye I watched as she nonchalantly dropped a few tubes of lipstick into one pocket, a compact and perfume into another. As we headed for the store exit, my heart pounded and I froze in my tracks when the security guard stopped us, even though I had stolen nothing. I knew her parents would take it with a grain of salt, but mine would be disgraced, and I would pay a heavy price. By a stroke of luck, I recognized the manager to be Quack's brother and implored him to let us go. He told us to get out and not come back. I almost wet my pants from the fright of it all and vowed I would never take something I couldn't pay for. It was a long time before I went near that store, and even then, I felt all eyes were on me as I browsed. After that incident, I didn't see much of my shoplifting friend. She had already moved on to a more exciting group.

Terrified as I was of shoplifting, my brother Jimmy recalls that sometimes it was a necessity. It meant the difference between eating lunch or not. When Dad would send him to the store with a dollar to buy things for his lunch the next day, he'd walk to Piggly Wiggly, steal the item, and get change for the dollar bill. He easily slipped a can of sardines or pack of cigarettes into the pockets of his bulky army jacket, assisted by deft fingers. There was no photo surveillance in the store aisles, and managers were usually occupied elsewhere. Returning home, he would give Dad the change, having deducted the cost of the pilfered item. The following day he was able to buy a bun and a slice of ham for lunch, washed down with a bottle of Coke.

My brother Bobby also saw some virtue in shoplifting as he related, "One day, me and Lechuga walked into the old Payless. He was one hell of a shoplifter. He always carried his coat or jacket over his left arm. He told me to walk in front, and as we exited the store, he put a radio under the coat. As we headed for the door, I heard a bunch of glass breaking. As we looked up, we realized the radio he was trying to steal was plugged in and the cord was dragging all the displays off the counter.

"Another time we were all standing on the southeast corner of the park and this lady driving by put her hand out to make a left turn signal. Lechuga yanked the wrist watch off her hand and we took off running. We later sold it for ten bucks. That same day we walked into the old Firestone Building on Don Gaspar, and Lechuga put a set of carving knives under his coat and one of the salesmen saw him. The guy asked him what he had put under his coat and he said, 'Nothing.' Then one of the knives fell out of the holder and stuck in the floor. The guy started laughing and we ran out of the store, without the knives, of course. Hell, we thought nothing about shoplifting, everything from cigarettes to candy bars. We sure didn't have money for anything, and we could go hungry if we didn't sneak something into our pockets."

Though not exactly an example of shoplifting, my brother Emilio once found a way to get food in an unusual manner. In the downtown area, there was a man who sold tamales out of a ten-pound bucket. When Emilio and his friend Tony Apodaca walked downtown, they'd usually meet up with this vendor around North De Vargas Street, near the bridge on the Santa Fe River. On one occasion, the tamale man struck up a conversation with them, and they told him they were going to the movies. Tony asked if he wanted a cigarette, and the man accepted the offer. Tony handed him a cigarette and offered to light it. After a few moments of idle conversation, the cigarette exploded, the surprised man dropped his tamale bucket, and with the diversion successfully created, the boys grabbed a handful of tamales and ran off toward town. Emilio mentioned that, as usual, they were delicious. A few months later, he learned that this vendor had been arrested for selling tamales made out of cat meat.

Some days we convinced ourselves that school was too boring, or our classroom was supervised by a substitute teacher who wouldn't take roll call. There was no point in ditching school because as we walked through the plaza we stuck out like sore thumbs since everyone else was in school. Nevertheless, teens still played hooky, some more than others. There were truant officers for each school district who showed no mercy. They could spot a ditcher from five hundred feet and seemed to be lurking at every corner. At some point we discovered that the truant officer whom we knew as Mr. Chávez was the brother of the local magistrate, so if you were caught by one, you would certainly be introduced to the other.

Although few of us liked the truant officers in general, sometimes there was good reason not to. Many times we heard whispered comments about a bespectacled and overweight truant officer who spent his time spying on teenagers in parked cars but never reported his activities to the school. Instead, he parked his vehicle near the local make-out place and quietly slithered up to the cars and peered through the steamy windows. In some instances he would get an eyeful of awkward teens experimenting with sex in the backseat. Many teens knew he did this regularly and could never look him in the eyes for fear he would recognize them. We heard all the sordid details of these encounters in the girls' bathroom, but due to fear of reprisal, his behavior couldn't be reported to the school. Nobody was brave enough to speak out against him, and besides, who would believe a teenager against an adult. And they'd have to admit that they were skipping school and engaging in other extracurricular activities.

In the mid-1940s, Grandpa Romero acquired a cigarette rolling machine. He bought the tobacco and papers and produced perfectly rolled cigarettes with this little machine. It wasn't uncommon for him to offer cigarettes to his grandchildren who were brave enough to take them. Some of the adults saw nothing wrong with smoking since long-term dangers were unknown. Grandpa's cigarettes were the real McCoy, not some sissified filtered cigarette. After trying her first cigarette, Cousin Ramona threw up all night and Grandma took her husband to task for encouraging youngsters to smoke.

But most of us didn't discover smoking until high school, and the habit was usually introduced by a friend, as in my case. From television and movies I learned how fashionable smoking appeared. I smoked my first cigarette at seventeen because I didn't want to seem unwilling or judgmental of my friends. I recall coughing and choking as I breathed in the bitter-tasting smoke. At lunchtime I watched boys lean casually against concrete walls, blowing large billows of smoke upward. The girls held their cigarettes daintily between fingers tipped with crimson nail polish. Cigarettes were sold everywhere, including at Payless, the five-and-dime store where you could buy two packs of Wings cigarettes for a quarter. Most brands such as Lucky Strike, Chesterfield, Camels, and an off-brand called One-Eleven were fifteen cents a pack. Phillip Morris cigarettes, which came in a brown wrapper, were extensively advertised on television, the ads showing a handsome young man dressed in a red bellhop uniform. Ads for Pall Mall cigarettes read "Reward yourself with the pleasure of smooth smoking; get smoothness, mildness, and satisfaction no other cigarette can offer." These seductive ads portrayed young people having fun while smoking, and most of us believed them.

As far as smoking was concerned, there were no official restrictions. Anybody could buy cigarettes, and anybody could smoke them. That is, until your parents got a whiff of your breath or clothing, and the lecture that followed was enough to discourage most teens. (Parents seemed to especially discourage girls from smoking.) We were foolish enough to believe that smoking was "cool," but I don't remember it being immediately addictive. I imagine I easily discarded it more from guilt than anything else. I recall standing near the open bathroom window at night and blowing smoke out through the screen. All the neighbors could probably see me, and I'm sure smoke slipped out under the door even when I placed a rolled towel against it. But I never got caught, maybe because my dad occasionally smoked and the odor remained for some time. My sister Rosalie often stood in the street talking to her friends, watching me blow smoke out the window, and threatened me with this damning evidence, but she never used it. As a young adult and an intermittent smoker, I never dared smoke around my mother, even though she suspected I smoked, having seen packages of cigarettes in my purse. I was embarrassed by my habit, and the message I thought it sent, and eventually I quit.

Many of us learned to drive at an early age, mostly by backing in and out of our driveways until we mastered the short distance without popping the clutch and killing the engine. The family car was generally reserved for working fathers and rarely driven by teenagers, except for emergencies and maybe for driving to the liquor store a few blocks away for a half pint of whiskey, handwritten note and ten-dollar bill in hand.

Few teens were prosperous enough to own cars. Occasionally someone in our circle of friends would drop out of high school and earn enough money working as a sack boy or laborer to afford a down payment on a car, often convincing his parents to cosign for the loan. Young owners drove some impressive cars down Cerrillos Road, and they tenderly maintained them. Every so often a car in the high school parking lot next to Seth Hall garnered the attention of everyone around. The focus was on a sizzling white 1940 Ford Convertible with red and yellow flames painted from the front of the hood to the back fenders. This baby had a massive V-8 engine, which sparkled like silver and purred like a mountain lion.

A 1956 Chevy Bel Air with chrome hubcaps and spinners that adorned the centers of wide, whitewall tires was surrounded by groups of admiring young teens. Teens had a separate lingo for the cars they modified. It included such terms as nosed, decked, shaved, filled, lowered, and Frenched, each referring to a process designed to beautify a vehicle, including removing the chrome parts, filling in the holes, sanding, and painting. These custom cars conjured up images of James Dean, black leather jackets, and slicked back hair, and their proud owners treated them with more tender love and respect than they had for any female. In his high school years, my brother Jimmy owned a royal blue 1956 Pontiac Star Chief flashing with chrome, chopped, channeled, nosed, and decked, with fender skirts and a lush, white leather interior. It had a V-8 engine with a two-barrel manifold and carbs. You could hear it coming for a mile. His favorite car was a '49 Mercury Coupe, a smooth, sleek baby of a car with every corner rounded. A pair of fuzzy, pink dice hung from the rearview mirror. Jimmy's nickname was "Jive," and the girls stood in line for a chance to ride with him. It was expensive for teens to maintain the upkeep on their cars, since there was little credit offered them. Jimmy purchased a set of tires on credit from Larragoite Tire, and when he missed a payment, the store took the tires back and left his car sitting on blocks in the driveway.

Some of the students either drove used cars with a few miles left on them or hand-me-down cars from parents or older siblings. Overall, cars were scarce, and when given the opportunity to cruise around Santa Fe, we took it. Gas cost less than twenty cents a gallon, and we'd put all our change together to buy a dollar's worth, which would last for a lot of miles. Since several of the boys from our group had dropped out of school in the eleventh grade, they would pick us up after school and take us on a slow cruise down Cerrillos Road to the hamburger joints where not only could we see, but also be seen. The loudspeakers blared Eddie Cochran's "Summertime Blues," and voices surged to be heard over the noise. There were lots of cars and lots of teenagers doing what they did best—just hanging out.

The menus at the drive-ins offered cheeseburgers, Cokes and milkshakes, French fries, hot dogs, and onion rings to satisfy our appetites whether we were hungry or not. Popular hangouts were Peterson's Drive-In on Pen Road and Bert's Drive-In and Ingram's Drive-In on Cerrillos Road. Bert's was closer in and has long since been converted to a flower shop. Ingram's was farther north past the Indian School and is now a used-car lot. Late nighters and coffee drinkers hung out after hours at Ly n' Bragg Truck Stop, a few miles farther north on Cerrillos Road, next to the Yucca Drive-In Theater, where after the movies we could have a Coke or a cup of coffee and sometimes even food.

Most girls stayed in school, and unless we were straight A students with scholarship potential, it appeared we were mostly primed to be either the secretaries or the mothers and housewives of tomorrow. Society assumed that we had no ambitions for life after high school, including college or any specific profession. Stereotypically, girls were encouraged to practice home arts via home economics classes, learning to sew aprons and bake scalloped potatoes and oatmeal cookies. A lot of young Betty Crockers were in the making. On the other side of the coin, Mrs. Kegel and Mrs. Blair taught typing, business practices, and shorthand, and at least we tried to master this mysterious language of curves and squiggles. Mrs. Kegel was a small, bespectacled teacher with silver-blue hair (on occasion close to a lavender color) and far past retirement age when I attended her classes. She had a way of clicking her tongue to make you aware that you weren't absorbing the subject matter and that you'd better start., since there would be few other options for us after graduation.

The local banks usually hired a few lucky female graduates and paid them about $160 per month as clerks, which factored out to about one dollar per hour. Most of these jobs lasted only until the girl married, since after all, she had been practicing all her life for that event. On my first job after high school, I quickly learned what being on the bottom rung of the ladder meant at the First National Bank. I performed the most menial of tasks as I attempted to learn the ropes. Several of us twiddled our thumbs most of the day and spent multiple breaks in the bathroom lounge downstairs. My job entailed posting figures for specific accounts on a daily basis. Many times there were as few as two entries per week, and the supervisor stood over my shoulder to make sure I entered them correctly. One day, while working through a lunch break, someone requested that I transfer funds from one bank to another using a key punch machine. I insisted I hadn't been shown how to do this but was assured it was very simple. I ended up transferring $100,000 instead of $10,000, and it wasn't discovered until later in the day when I inquired about where to file the transaction copies. After that, the supervisor in the Trust Department started watching new employees a little more closely.

After working at the bank for more than six months, the rows of figures began to blur before my eyes causing me to suffer regularly from severe migraine headaches. The supervisor shook her head, commenting that most people had headaches and it never interfered with their work. I decided then to reevaluate my career choice, particularly when I realized I was not mature enough to overlook what I considered to be prejudicial treatment of Spanish-surnamed people. I happily went on to explore a career as a legal secretary, one that would serve me for the next twenty years.

Chapter Sixteen

A Sense of Fashion

As children, we were mostly oblivious to our clothing as long as we were warm in the winter and cool in the summer. When our shoes wore down and holes appeared in the soles, we placed a cardboard tracing of the sole inside the shoe so it could be worn just a little bit longer...maybe until the next paycheck, maybe until the next birthday. As teens, our clothes were on the conservative side, but we tried to mimic styles we saw in teen magazines.

My sister Rosalie was one grade ahead of me all through school and was my best friend. In high school, when we both met friends closer to our ages, we only spent time together at home. As with many sisters, sometimes there was tension between us, but at home we were true siblings. During her senior year at Santa Fe High School in 1958, she was employed by Hubbard's Department Store, on the plaza where Price-Dewey Gallery is today, receiving a welcome weekly paycheck. Suddenly she could afford to buy her own clothes, and lots of them. At every opportunity I slipped her neat clothes on under my jacket, but she usually caught me sometime during the day, usually in the girl's bathroom, and she would raise hell then and later when we got home. I fondly remember a fuzzy, pink angora sweater that I had slipped out of her drawer and wore under my coat, not bothering to ask her permission. Even though it looked far better on her than it did on me, I still coveted my sister's sweater and rest of her wardrobe.

In my early teen years my clothes never seemed right. I didn't know why, but I felt they were different. Maybe it was because everything but our underwear was homemade from inexpensive fabric and the material faded over months of washing. Some of the higher-end stores downtown such as La Tienda filled their windows with mannequins dressed in felt skirts of all colors decorated with sequins and poodle appliqués. Because of our almost nonexistent clothes budget, we could only be fashion conscious to a limited degree. We wore layers and layers of net petticoats under our mostly homemade skirts, stiffened every few days with heavy starch or with a mixture of sugar and water. Rosalie's drawer housed one of these coveted pink, flared felt skirts adorned with appliquéd black poodles wearing rhinestone collars on their necks. Every teen needed a cardigan sweater with a matching pullover, a pleated skirt, plenty of silk scarves, and more than one cinch belt. Girls usually wore flats (shoes without heels), penny loafers, and saddle shoes. Fuzzy, pastel-colored angora sweaters were the rage of the season. Mannequins in Bell's Department Store windows were dressed in Capri pants and pedal pushers, and halter tops or blouses with Peter Pan collars, but we could afford none of this. I don't recall wearing trousers or jeans until my late teens, when pedal pushers and Capri pants were becoming fashionable.

The cloth from the skirts and blouses we outgrew was recycled and cut into squares to make quilts for our beds, since there were no other female children left to hand them down to. As adults years later, Rosalie and I would recognize a square on one of Mother's quilts, remembering the skirt or blouse we had worn in school, amazed at how a particular green paisley material survived through the years.

Rosalie and I weren't allowed to wear lipstick but would quickly apply it on the way to school, stopping at the first side mirror of a parked car, or we'd run into the school bathroom and stand on tiptoe in front of the mirror where every other girl was jostling for space. Sometimes one of us would forget to wipe it off after school, and sitting at the dinner table we signaled each other with exaggerated gestures until one of us realized that we were eating soup through ruby-stained lips, wondering if our parents had noticed. I'm sure Mother did, but she never said anything.

I would guess that the Santa Fe I knew was not part of mainstream America when it came to fashion trends. None of my friends or relatives wore clothing such as we saw on *American Bandstand*, which, even if it was available in local stores, was far too expensive. During each intermission on television, we viewed commercials for lipstick, makeup, and hair spray that were not yet on the shelves of stores in our area.

Back then there was little or no focus on weight. You were the size you were, and clothes were purchased to fit that size. Overweight and underweight teens fit into the same niche as everyone else. Even some of the teen idols carried extra pounds. It was not as big a deal as it is today.

Rosalie and I slept in the same bed for most of our growing-up years, and she always opted to sleep near the wall where it was cooler. Since the house was adobe, it was cool in the summer and warm in the winter. We spent hours reading our favorite teen magazines before bedtime, including *Photoplay*, *Modern Screen*, and *Teen World*. Through these we entered the world of fantasy and make-believe. We went to bed each night with hair rolled up with rag curlers, made from metal strips cut from tomato sauce cans and wrapped with pieces of cotton cloth. Between these nightly curlers and daytime bobby pins, we fashioned fairly respectable hairdos, especially after we combed out our hair and sprayed it down with a few layers of Aqua Net hair spray. Girls wore their hair mostly pulled back in ponytails, and boys cut their hair in flat tops or crew cuts, until the mid-1950s when Elvis Presley sported the hairdo everyone tried to mimic, sideburns and all.

My one-day career as a fashion model came to a quick demise on graduation day from Harrington Junior High. After a great deal of shopping, I had finally chosen *the dress*, a $19.95 or less special from Montgomery Ward, with sheer, flocked pink fabric over a full taffeta skirt and short cap sleeves. I knew how many groceries that amount would buy, and I was grateful, choosing inexpensive white pumps to complement the outfit.

Early that afternoon I bathed and dressed in anticipation of looking no less than spectacular for the day's ceremonies. Milling around in the gym's dressing room nervously chatting, the other students and I did our final primping. As each student was called to the stage to receive their diploma, to my great surprise and disappointment I discovered that another classmate had chosen the same pink dress for the occasion.

Unfortunately, since her name was closer to the beginning of the alphabet, her dress was seen first. Mary Lou Elmore was a taller and bigger girl than I was, but that didn't alter the design of the dress. It was the same and I was in distress. When I heard my name, I couldn't move fast enough across the stage to grab my diploma, curtsy, and dash back to my folding chair, hoping no one had noticed. Graduation wasn't celebrated with a party, so I returned home afterward to bask alone in the glory.

Of the seven children in my family, only Rosalie, Ricardo, and I graduated from both junior high and high school.

Chapter Seventeen

ROCKING AROUND THE CLOCK

When my mother and her sister Sally were young adults, they learned to dance the Charleston, a dance craze that swept through the country in the mid-1920s. In 1925 they attended a movie at the Lensic Theater, *King on Main Street*, where actress Bessie Love introduced the dance to the young audience. Living with relatives in Santa Fe, the girls rushed home to try the dance steps. Aunt Sally recalled that after an exhausting hour of perfecting their dance routine to the music of a scratched vinyl record played on their old hand-cranked wind-up Victrola, they would fall to the floor laughing.

Later on my parents occasionally caught the dancing bug too. They were members of the Fraternal Order of Eagles, still in existence today as a social drinking club. They attended dances regularly at the Odd Fellows Hall between the cemetery on Cerrillos Road and Baca Street, where the meetings were held. Some of my fondest memories of them as a couple are when they would get all dressed up, Mom in her ruffled skirt and blouse, and Dad in his Western shirt and pants, and they would

Sally and Senaida
Ortega, Santa Fe, 1927.

go square dancing. They practiced the steps in the living room at home, and I remembered the words "aleman left," but I never knew what they meant. Just watching them twirl around the living room floor was enough of a treat.

But in the 1950s teens listened to a variety of music. Back then there were no Walkmans, so radios were limited to table-top models, a console with a record player, or a car radio, if you had occasion to be in a car. Music ranged from Dean Martin's "Memories Are Made of This," Mitch Miller and his band with "Yellow Rose of Texas," and Tennessee Ernie Ford with "Sixteen Tons," to Pat Boone's "Love Letters in the Sand." A Latino band led by Perez Prado recorded a popular instrumental, "Cherry Pink and Apple Blossom White," which spent a long time on the popularity charts. Eddie Fisher starred as host of the *Coca-Cola Hour* on radio, singing "Oh! My Papa." His face appeared on the cover of every teen magazine from *Photoplay* to *Hollywood Secrets*. He wasn't particularly drop-dead handsome but apparently represented someone's idea of America's clean-cut boy next door. Dean Martin sang "That's Amore," Perry Como cautioned "Don't Let the Stars Get in Your Eyes," and Patti Page barked "(How Much Is) That Doggie in the Window?"

Sometime around 1956, rock and roll blasted into our lives. The explosion included Elvis Presley, who debuted early in the year with "Heartbreak Hotel," along with Little Richard, Chuck Berry, Jerry Lee Lewis, Buddy Holly, Fats Domino, and a bevy of others. All of a sudden everything around us changed. Car radios blared, bringing the sound of music to the streets. We were completely overcome, mesmerized, and music permeated the senses in every spare moment. This was no ordinary music that we could whistle on the way to school, no catchy tune sung with an orchestra in the background. We were caught up in the pulsating rhythm, so unlike the traditional music we were accustomed to. We tapped our feet and swayed our hips as we sang along with Buddy Knox and "Party Doll" and grooved to the rhythms of The Ventures, instrumental music that needed no words...we got the message. Chubby Checker's hips gyrated to "The Twist," a dance that even teenagers with two left feet could move to. Other songs like "Lipstick on Your Collar," "Stupid Cupid," and "My Boyfriend's Back" caught the attention of teens everywhere.

In my small world it appeared that most teenagers in Santa Fe never reached the pulsating perfection displayed on *American Bandstand*, the Dick Clark show that aired on television every Saturday. Unlike scenarios portrayed on television and in the movies, teenagers wearing penny loafers and bobby sox didn't groove to the music blaring from a jukebox at the soda parlors in Santa Fe, at least not in my neighborhood. They mostly sat and listened at tables with small jukebox selectors where music could be chosen and paid for right at the table. School dances were lively, and those who knew the latest dance steps could strut their stuff, bopping and jitterbugging to the pulsating rhythms. I, for one, was too shy to ask anyone to teach me how to dance, and my brothers were far too busy socializing with their friends to notice.

Johnnie Ray slowed the pace a little with "Just Walkin' in the Rain," followed by Elvis with "A Fool Such as I," and we even listened to such banal numbers as "Kookie, Kookie, Lend Me Your Comb," from the television program, 77 *Sunset Strip. The Ed Sullivan Show* was a weekly event. He showcased all the teen heartthrobs—Fabian, Frankie Avalon, and Mousketeer Annette Funicello, whether they could carry a tune or not. We now followed the Top 20, and bought '45 and '78 records at the Santa Fe Music Store on Marcy Street with every spare cent we could get our hands on. And, of course, Elvis was King. We listened to the radio deep into the night, kept the volume down low enough to not disturb our parents, and fell asleep to the sounds of KOMA-Oklahoma running through the airwaves. For those who were lucky enough to have access to cars, the music blared loudly from rolled down windows, even in the wintertime.

One of the local radio stations had a disc jockey with a dreamy voice that slid out over the radio waves. All the girls swooned over him, a captive audience of dreamy-eyed young virgins imagining him to be tall, dark, and handsome. His mellow voice exuded a sex appeal generally lacking in the local denizens. The station had a call-in line that was always busy, and talking to him for even a moment was a thrill. In my dreams I imagined him to be at least six foot tall, green-eyed, handsome, and sexy. Introduced at a high school assembly one spring, much to my dismay he wasn't much taller than most of the boys in our class, was a little homely looking, and wore large, horn-rimmed glasses. It took a while to recover from the shock, and listening to the radio wasn't half as much fun after that bubble had been burst.

In high school all the girls obsessed about senior prom late in the springtime. I considered myself too much of a wallflower to even imagine being asked to any of the dances, especially by a *senior.* Not only was I inexperienced in the ways of romance, I was sixteen and had never been noticed, touched, or spoken to, let alone kissed. The only time I attended a school dance was in seventh grade, and that's because it was held in the afternoon. I didn't know how to dance. I spent the entire week before practicing dance steps on a magazine advertising chart—you know, the one with the footprints—one, two, three, four, not realizing they were just an illustration and not actual steps to any specific dance. That afternoon, a fellow classmate asked me to dance. He was a little on the chubby side and had very sweaty hands, so wet that he spent most of his time wiping them on the side of his pants. I confidently walked onto the dance floor with him and remember counting to myself. I couldn't help noticing some of the boys on the sidelines scratching their heads, probably thinking, *What the heck is she doing?* Needless to say, my career as a popular, sought-out dancing partner was short-lived (a fact that would follow me through adulthood). Dancing was like riding a bike—if you didn't learn it at a young age and had no reason to do it, it became harder to master as years went by.

So the senior prom was only a distant fantasy, even though I might have enjoyed listening to rock and roll music played by one of the local bands. When asked the inevitable question, "Are you going to the prom?" I offered various excuses: "We're going out of town," "I'm coming down with a cold," or "My folks won't let me," rather than the true one, "I wasn't asked, but neither were most sophomores." But "my folks won't let me" also rang true in my case. My dad was so strict that the only places we were actually allowed to go to were church, school, and on occasion, down to the liquor store to fetch a six pack of beer. Any other request got "No, so don't ask"—and if by some remote chance my sister and I caught him off guard and he said we could attend a football game, we had to be home by ten anyway, or there would be hell to pay.

Chapter Eighteen

COMMUNITY CELEBRATIONS

Santa Fe summers ended each year with two simultaneous celebrations: the burning of Zozobra, Old Man Gloom, followed by the Santa Fe Fiesta, both held over Labor Day weekend. Some of the younger kids believed that this Zozobra figure was like La Llorona, the legendary bogeywoman. However, the huge figure, a giant paper puppet standing more than fifty feet high, was designed and created in 1926 by Santa Fe artist Will Shuster, one of the original *Los Cinco Pintores* (a group of artists who were responsible for establishing Santa Fe as an art colony), and was constructed annually by hundreds of volunteers who built its big-headed wooden framework and covered it with layers of paper. It had dangling, articulated arms that moved up and down, as did its mouth, and its movements were controlled much like those of a marionette.

The event was held on the grounds of Fort Marcy Park a few blocks north of the plaza, past the Masonic Temple, a large, pink, castle-like building on the north side of Santa Fe on Bishop's Lodge Road. Spectators could drive their cars up to

Zozobra figure.
Courtesy New Mexico
State Records Center
and Archives,
Department of
Tourism Collection
No. 2482.

the burning site and sit on the car hood enjoying a picnic.
Preparation for the event built into a frenzy, and as soon as the
sun began to set, dancers appeared and began chanting and
cavorting around the figure. For more than twenty years,
Jacques Cartier, one of Santa Fe's well-known celebrities and
the lead dancer at these festivities, was handed a lighted torch
and after much swaying, spinning, tempting, and cajoling, he
set the giant ablaze. In the darkness, as the massive figure
burned from the bottom up, it erupted into a shower of brilliant fireworks, and then began to moan and groan loudly. Even
if you weren't watching it in person, you could still hear these
eerie sounds for miles away. One of the purposes of the event
was for people to burn their problems along with Zozobra.
People chanted in tandem, *burn, burn,* as the figure burned to
ashes. When the fire died down to embers, everyone walked or

drove down the hill to the plaza, where the Santa Fe Fiesta would officially begin.

My father recalled that as a young man the burning of Zozobra was held in the parking lot behind City Hall and the figure was only about twenty feet tall. "Some of the men had firearms and would shoot bullets into the figure and then bonfires around it were ignited and the figure was burned to cinders, which in turn set off the fireworks stored inside. Then the chanting crowd formed a giant conga line around the still burning figure and sang and danced to 'La Cucaracha' until it burned down to ashes." They continued the merriment on the way to the plaza, where they stopped first at the food booths and then wound their way to the lounge of the La Fonda Hotel for a drink.

The Santa Fe Fiesta, or Fiestas, began each year in late August or early September with a solemn procession from St. Francis Cathedral to Rosario Cemetery several blocks away. Six men transported the historical statue of La Conquistadora on an ornate carrier made of wood and metal. This statue dated back to the days when Don Diego de Vargas and his soldiers returned her to Santa Fe. (A major figure in New Mexico history, De Vargas reconquered Santa Fe in 1692 after the Pueblo Revolt of 1680 forced the Spaniards to flee.) They prayed to this statue for success in battle against the Indians. Fiestas were a three-day celebration, with continuous entertainment provided by mariachi bands, singers, and dancers, with an array of food sold from small wooden booths. The green chile burgers and tamales, along with corn on the cob, were in great demand by the hungry crowd. One or two booths sold paper cones filled with sugary pink fluffs of cotton candy, which melted in your mouth on contact. On Saturday mornings, there was a Pet Parade, the *desfile de los niños*, when children dressed as animals walked or rode on wagons while accompanied by their gaily dressed dogs, cats, donkeys, rabbits, and other pets, and by their parents who also dressed as animals. The Historical/Hysterical Parade featured people wearing costumes, some in decorated floats, poking fun at politicians, city fathers, or recent events in the local news.

On the final Sunday, the main fiesta parade centered on colorfully decorated floats carrying the Fiesta queen and her court.

Santa Fe Fiesta,
1954, Marie
and former
sister-in-law.

Chosen months earlier from a bevy of young Santa Fe beauties
who had met all the requirements of the Fiesta Council, these
young women represented local groups and organizations. A few
young men were also chosen from entrants to portray Don Diego
de Vargas and his court. The floats were followed by the Rodeo
Queen and Indian princesses on horseback. Every day during
Fiestas bands played, songs were sung, and people danced happily in the streets. The celebration ended with a procession from
Rosario Chapel back to the cathedral, returning the statue of La
Conquistadora to a perch high on the altar of her chapel.

Although my older siblings probably attended Fiestas on their
own, my sister and I anxiously anticipated our parents' invitation.
Every year Mother purchased many yards of brightly colored cotton material and lovingly sewed beautiful fiesta skirts for us,
trimmed with equally bright rows of rickrack. The white ruffled

Santa Fe Fiesta Queen Anita Romero and her court, 1949. Rosalie second row on right.

blouses she sewed had puffed sleeves and were accentuated with equal amounts of bright rickrack and ribbon. We walked with glee toward the center of town to join in the celebration.

In 1949 my oldest sister Anita was chosen to be the Santa Fe Fiesta Queen, to reign over that year's Fiesta activities. She was the most beautiful of them all. We were all proud, but my parents were beaming at the sight of their radiant daughter. My sister Rosalie was chosen to serve in her court as a page and participated in all the Fiesta activities that year dressed in a velvet uniform, with her hair turned under in a page-boy.

Later that year, we learned that the queen's float from the Santa Fe Fiesta had been invited to the Rose Bowl Parade in Pasadena, California. This was the only time in the history of the Fiesta that such an honor was bestowed on the city. The Rose Bowl took place in January of 1950, and we were glued to Grandma's television set as we tried to catch a glimpse of the Santa Fe float.

Rose Bowl Parade, 1950, Santa Fe Fiesta float.

Coinciding with Fiestas, a large carnival with merry-go-rounds and Ferris wheels was usually held on the outer edges of the city. Mostly teenagers and young adults frequented the carnival, as many older adults believed carnivals were evil places where shrewd games were designed to steal the hard-earned money of the working class. Many paychecks were lost by a young man foolishly trying to impress his girlfriend. The carnival workers would let them win at these games of chance once or twice, convince them that in the next few times they could really win big, and then take all their money.

There were lights everywhere—on all the rides and on all the booths. Even the poles in between had lights that sparkled from every direction, which made it even more exciting. We usually went in a group of as many as could fit in a car. After purchasing tickets for rides, we stood in line. The Tilt-A-Wheel started slowly, and I thought to myself, *Oh, this isn't so bad.* But within seconds everything sped up and it scared the hell out of me. The ride paused when it reached its highest point and then plummeted down. I thought I was dead for sure. I white-knuckled it, holding my breath so I wouldn't scream and let everyone know how frightened I was. After a while, the popularity of the carnivals waned, and they became smaller as the years went by.

Most of the Spanish people in Santa Fe, including my parents, attended the annual *Baile de los Cascarones* sponsored by La Sociedad Folklórica, a group of women dedicated to preserving New Mexican folklore and traditions. This event began in 1940 and usually took place on Shrove Tuesday (*El martes de carnestolendas*), the Tuesday before Ash Wednesday. In New Orleans, it is celebrated as Fat Tuesday or Mardi Gras. The dance represented the last opportunity for revelry and indulgence in food and drink before Lent, the forty-day period of self-denial and abstinence.

Hollowed-out chicken eggs were accumulated for months to prepare for the baile. (Everyone ate a lot of scrambled eggs and custard in that time period.) Mother taught us to pierce the top and bottom of a raw egg with a pin or needle. In order to force the egg yolk out of the shell, we carefully increased the size of the bottom hole and blew the egg contents into a bowl from the top. After the eggshell dried, we carefully placed it in a basket. When we collected a sufficient number, we meticulously filled the shells with confetti made from tiny shreds of colored paper, cut by hand or bought in ready-to-use packages from the five-and-dime store. Before stuffing the confetti into the eggshell, we lightly sprayed it with perfume, and we sealed the hole with a thin piece of tissue paper dipped into glue made from flour and water. Thus these paper-filled eggshells were transformed into cascarones. We colorfully decorated the eggs with paints or egg dye, many of them with faces and geometric designs. I loved to paint these faces, with big eyes, fuzzy eyebrows, and long handlebar moustaches.

At the dance, couples purchased the cascarones for twenty-five cents each to crack them over the head of the person with whom they wished to dance. It was customary to never refuse a dance with the person holding an egg. Many of the women wore brilliant, traditional dresses lovingly preserved and handed down by their female ancestors, their hair piled gracefully high and secured with a vintage tortoise-shell comb adorned by a lace mantilla that cascaded down the sides of their faces. Dad dressed in black pants, a bell-sleeved, white satin shirt, and red cummerbund around his waist; Mom wore a three-tiered broom skirt with a colorfully embroidered white peasant blouse, since her ancestors hadn't owned expensive dresses worthy of preservation. After the dance they brought home a basket of decorated eggs, and we eventually smashed them on each other's heads, jumping and laughing the entire time.

On weekends during the early years of their marriage, my parents attended dances at the Old Armory of the Soldiers on Washington Avenue where the Fray Angélico Chávez History Library is today. Men were charged seventy-five cents admission, and since no liquor was served, they could bring a bottle of liquor or beer to the event. The music was gay and rhythmic, mostly polkas that originated from the small Army bands who entertained the soldiers north of Santa Fe at Fort Marcy in the late 1800s. At Quintana's Dance Hall on the corner of Galisteo and Alameda Streets, near the M&M Grocery Store, couples danced into the night. One of the more popular dance hall sites was the Elías Dance Hall on Camino del Monte Sol at the corner of Acequia Madre Street, just to the right of Canyon Road. Here weddings, baptisms, and other social gatherings were held for the Spanish population of the area. My father recalled that in 1932, the Depression reached Santa Fe, and for the next seven to eight years its effects permeated the region. "During those years, there was little money to be spent on entertainment and most of the dance halls closed." However, traditional New Mexican music continued to flourish, since family celebrations were still held, although on a smaller scale.

With the advent of World War II, the old dance halls were replaced by taverns, saloons, honky-tonks, and bars all over Santa Fe and north of the city. These establishments had a different atmosphere than the dance halls, and Mother felt out of place among all the noise, smoke, alcohol, and the sometimes brazen women. The most popular of these were the Plaza Bar in downtown Santa Fe; George King's—one of the most notorious of the bars; and the El Fidel Hotel Bar, which featured traditional New Mexican music played by two or three musicians on Saturday nights. And dances were still enjoyed at weekend gatherings for weddings and baptisms, readily attended by all those invited. My parents danced at those, and Grandpa Albert twirled the younger children around to the sounds of clapping hands and tapping feet, introducing us to the music of our culture. This music was usually performed by a small group with a guitar, violin, and accordion. It was rhythmic and cheery, and the steps were easily learned. The musicians usually alternated waltzes and polkas so the couples could catch their breath between dances.

Chapter Nineteen

DARK HOURS

Although growing up in Santa Fe seemed fairly uneventful most of the time, as teenagers we experienced our share of tragedies. Even if we were not personally involved in an event, we were affected nonetheless.

Emilio often accompanied his friend Art Frank on trips around Santa Fe delivering telegrams for Western Union. He recalls going along to deliver thirteen telegrams to families notifying them of their sons' deaths in combat during the Korean War.

Jimmy's best friend throughout high school years, Leroy, drowned in a boating accident when the boat he was fishing from at Santa Cruz Lake capsized. Our Aunt Mela died suddenly, leaving our teenage cousin Gilbert to grow up without a mother. And a schoolmate of ours in junior high, one of the young Peña boys, died from leukemia.

The most dramatic tragedy occurred when a young classmate in junior high went missing one winter morning and after a week was presumed to be a runaway. Many stories circulated

about her sudden disappearance, ranging from speculation that
she ran away to rumors that she had been kidnapped. Some
months later, after the winter thaw, the car she had been driving
was found in a ravine near Los Alamos, about thirty-five miles
from Santa Fe. She had apparently swerved off the icy road, land-
ing in such an obscure place that the car couldn't be seen from
the road.

When our cousin Virginia died as a young adult, we peered
from the windows as the Martínez family, dressed in black,
entered their cars to attend the funeral. For us, a terrible mystery surrounded the death of someone so young. We knew she
had suffered with an unexplained illness most of her young life,
but we never expected God to snatch someone from among us.
With each death of a classmate or relative, the realities of life
loomed over our heads.

When I was five, I wandered over to Grandma Romero's,
likely hungry or simply in need of attention. I entered the house
through the back door and meandered into the kitchen. Finding
no one there, I walked into the dining room and then back
through the kitchen, around to the bedroom, and admired
Grandma's big, four-poster brass bed covered with a colorful,
puffy quilt. Not a thing out of place. There still wasn't anyone
around, so I skipped down the short, narrow hallway past the
bathroom and wondered why the door to the living room was
closed; it darkened the hallway more than usual. Opening the
door, I bounced into the room and came to a quick halt. There in
the corner of the living room entrance was Mama Vía, lying very
still and quiet in a long wooden box, her hands folded at her
waist, her crystal rosary sparkling in the sunlight reflected from
the glass entry door. As I walked over to her, in addition to the
eerie silence in the room, I noticed no movement at all, her eyes
closed, and her hands oddly still as they prayed. Thinking she
was asleep and that I would get in trouble for waking her, I gently poked her shoulder and asked for Grandma Anastasia. At that
moment, I heard the kitchen door close and steps come toward
me, and I looked up to see Grandma whisk into the room in a
huff, scolding me for being there. She reached over to pull me
toward her, scaring me even more, and I flew out of the house

and ran back home. I never saw Mama Vía again, and I never knew where she went. It seemed like old people simply disappeared one day and adults never explained why. Maybe this was the reason why I was always afraid of the dark, imagining that I too would be whisked off into the night, never to be seen again.

As children we were never allowed to attend funerals, since we were never informed when someone died. Although Rosario Cemetery had been in use since the early 1800s, the Guadalupe Cemetery was the burial place of many of our early ancestors. It was located at the end of Calle Grillo, off Early Street, a few blocks west of our neighborhood. At the edge of a small hill surrounded by lilac bushes and a short wire fence, there were many old grave sites. Our great-grandfather was buried there, along with Grandma's brother, Tío Narciso. She would visit his grave often, particularly on Memorial Day, but it was a place we thought was off-limits without a parent accompanying us.

I noticed that in some families, death wasn't such a mystery and was observed out in the open. The Tapia family down the block held a wake in the front yard, placing the small pine coffin of their tiny baby girl on a table. She was dressed in white, and the reflection of the coins on her eyes sparkled in the sunlight. We watched this eerie celebration from the safety of our yard, not wanting to get too close, yet fascinated by every detail.

My cousin Peppy Rivera, who lived on Daniel Street on the other side of town near Rosario Cemetery, recalled a similar experience. The family who lived in the rental next door had an infant who died shortly after birth, and as people gathered at the house for the funeral, the mother placed the small casket on the porch wall and went back into the house. Meanwhile, Peppy wandered over and opened what she believed was simply a pretty white box and discovered a beautiful, doll-like baby outfitted in a white lace cap and dress. As she reached to pick the baby up, the baby's mother came running out of the house, screaming. Startled, Peppy dropped the lid of the casket and ran home, where Aunt Sally gave her a good chewing out.

Mother recalled that during her childhood in Ojo de la Vaca, wakes were held in the home of the deceased and lasted the entire night. "After the coffin was purchased from the *carpintero* and delivered to the house, it was propped up on two wooden saw-horses. The relatives had the task of preparing the body for burial, which included bathing, dressing, fixing hair, and adding a touch of makeup. Once this was done, the body was lovingly placed in the coffin, which had been lined with whatever materials were available. Relatives and neighbors brought prepared foods to the home and placed them on the kitchen table. Each person who entered the home gave their condolences, *el pésame*, to members of the family, including children who might be present.

"After condolences were given, everyone sat on chairs and benches set up for the wake. In the evening a rosary was recited led by a *rezador*, hired to lead the prayers. After one or several rosaries, the food was served. Adults took turns praying and sitting with the body all night. The women dressed in all black, with black shawls draped over their heads. The next day, the coffin was placed in the back of the truck and taken to the church where the funeral Mass was held. At the cemetery, there was little pomp and ceremony. The priest said a few prayers, sprinkled holy water on the coffin, and departed from the scene. Everyone returned to the home for a meal and to talk about how wonderful the *defunto* [the deceased] had been during his lifetime."

Chapter Twenty

BRUJAS, EL DIABLO, AND OLD WIVES TALES

During the Lenten season, which began on Ash Wednesday, my family's custom was to visit all the Catholic churches in our town and to sacrifice something special for the forty days until Easter. During this period we attempted to be better people, at least at home. I usually gave up bubble gum and sometimes, to appear more pious, included an item I didn't eat much of anyway, like cream puffs. On Good Friday we weren't allowed to do anything during the three hours of the Passion, not even listen to the radio or watch television, especially if we hadn't gone to church for the afternoon services, which meant sitting in a pew, preferably in the back of the church, from noon to three o'clock.

Mother frequently related stories and offered warnings to keep us on the right side of the tracks during Lent, and at the time, we trusted their veracity. She recalled that she and her sister Sally, while living in Ojo de la Vaca, were drawn to the music coming from an old dance hall on a long-ago, dark Good Friday evening. The sun had barely set as they departed from the house, telling Mama Inés they were going next door to play with their cousins. Fifteen minutes later, shivering with excitement, they crept up to the windows of the dance hall and looked in to see what was unfolding within. According to my mother, "It was just a one-room dance hall. It was filled with thick smoke, so much that it hung like a curtain from the ceiling down. *Los músicos* were sitting in old wood chairs on a stage raised about a foot from the ground. First they played a soft valse, and then a quick polka. We tapped our feet and swayed our hips to the music as we stood on the mound of dirt near the window. Sally and I sure wanted to get in there and dance, but Mama would have skinned us alive."

I found it comforting that her generation had similar rules for Lent and Good Friday that we did. It assured me there was something to the religion. She continued with the story, "Everybody was all dressed up, you'd have thought it was Easter Sunday. The women were *todas perfumadas*, with lipstick and rouged cheeks. They wore high-heeled shoes and nylons, and their jewelry rattled as they danced. The music got louder and louder, and everybody was drinking and dancing. You could hear the laughter right above the music. Then, a tall, handsome man stepped into the room. Oh, he was good looking! He had dark, wavy hair that formed small curls at his neck, and these piercing dark eyes that sparkled any time light hit them. He must have walked right by us, but we didn't see him. All the ladies swooned as he took them out, one by one, to the center of the dance floor, spinning and twirling them to the enchanting rhythms of the music. Sally and I watched, thinking we should go in and join the festivities, and we had almost talked ourselves into it, but we sure knew better."

Mom also described the way the women's dresses spun as they twirled around to the tempo of the music, and then continued, "Well, this man kept dancing with all the women, and their *viejos* were sitting at the bar, glaring at them while they sputtered and giggled in delight, coyly fluttering their eyelashes. Suddenly, one of the women let out an ear-piercing scream! Holding her hand over her mouth in horror, she pointed to the mysterious stranger's feet! As they all looked down, they saw his hooves, and then a pointed tail slowly emerged from under his jacket! In the middle of the screaming, everyone headed for the door but they couldn't open it. It was shut tight. One of the men ran over and kicked it open, and the smoke tumbled out the door in waves as if propelled by a strong wind. Sally and I turned and ran home and never looked back. We couldn't imagine what would have happened if we'd gone in there. *Dios mio!* When we got home, Mama said we looked like we had seen a ghost. We said nothing and jumped under the covers, clothes and all! The moral to the story was that if you're going to do something forbidden on Good Friday, *el diablo* won't be too far behind." Of course, as children we were always careful not to break any of the Lenten rules, since Mother repeated the story every year, embellishing it each time with a subtle new twist.

Another story Mother told served to increase my fear of outdoor bathrooms. "When I was growing up," she said, "your Grandma Inés told us to be very careful going out at night, because there were unexplainable events that happened in the darkness. At one of the old houses in Pecos there appeared *una bola de lumbre*, a big ball of fire that rolled around the house like a tumbleweed, out to *el excusado*, the outdoor bathroom, circling it several times. Of course this happened on a night when the moon went behind the clouds and the sky was very dark. The occupants of the house stood shivering behind the closed curtains, peeking through the corners out into the yard. The fireball was said to be the spirit of an old hag who was killed by a pack of dogs as she was going to the outhouse. Her father had sold her soul for a lot of money many years before when she was a child, and the dogs were sent to claim it. She ran in every direction, screaming her head off, until the dogs finally attacked and killed her. So every so often, when the nights were particularly dark, she would come to haunt the house where her family had lived, circling and screaming the whole time."

We had little difficulty believing stories we were told. Most of the adults we knew were superstitious, and they believed the old stories their grandparents told them. Dad was particularly superstitious. He wouldn't eat food prepared by a pregnant woman, regardless if she was a relative. I never understood the origins of this particular fallacy. His theory was that if he did, he would become infected with a disease. Mother had undergone seven pregnancies during their marriage, so this particular oddity must have begun as he aged, because he readily ate the meals she prepared all during their marriage.

People had other beliefs too, such as if a woman was pregnant, she wasn't allowed to thread a needle because she might contract an infection somehow and die. We were also told that certain people had the power to cast spells, and if a hex befell you, your life would go downhill from there. I wasn't sure how this would be accomplished.

In later years, Mother believed that her sister Sally had been a victim of *mal ojo*, the evil eye, while sitting at one of the downtown cafés. Sally was always a good-natured person, happy-go-lucky and generally busy raising her family on Daniel Street, near West San Francisco Street. My mother and her sister met often for lunch at a downtown eatery, where they would talk and laugh for hours. One day after eating lunch, Sally's life changed drastically, and she became nervous and withdrawn. She rarely visited our family anymore and began spending long hours in her bedroom, staring at the walls. The sisters never met for lunch again because her illness became severe as the years passed. We visited her often, but after a while, she became reclusive, never venturing out of the house. Her once nicely coiffed black hair was now almost completely white and matted because she didn't want anyone to touch her. This crushed my mother; it was as if her sister was gone, even though she was still alive. Years later she was diagnosed with Alzheimer's disease, and her devoted family cared for her until her death. When I'm walking around in downtown Santa Fe, I make it a point to cross the street when I approach this café, always remembering the things my mother said about it. Somewhere deep down in my heart I didn't believe in superstition, but the fact that my mother believed this made just that much difference. For years I believed that you would be able to tell who could give you mal ojo because surely there would be something noticeable about their eyes.

Epilogue

Until my senior year in high school I had several best friends, mostly girls, but never a boyfriend. Since I had skipped third grade, I was younger than my fellow students and therefore not "date" material. This dilemma was coupled with the fact that my parents were extremely strict, but the issue went deeper than that. In some respects I was somewhat mature, but I was completely inexperienced in the more worldly aspects of life, and that included relationships with the opposite sex.

We never talked about sex. Maybe Mom figured my sister and I were better off not knowing. I was very immature for my age, sheltered and protected from most things outside our walls, especially anything to do with our bodies. Dad did not allow us to wear shorts or halter tops, even on the hottest of days. He considered it unladylike but seemed to enjoy seeing other women walking downtown in the attire forbidden to us. In school, I blushed overhearing a classmate talk so freely about matters that were never discussed at home.

But in 1959 at Santa Fe High, I finally had a real boyfriend. Although I was unprepared to share myself or my thoughts with anyone, I did a fairly good job of playacting. If this was love, I certainly wouldn't have recognized it. There was no handbook to follow, so I followed my instincts, which were usually wrong. I became a young lady with several hats to wear: daughter, sibling, student, and girlfriend.

My first boyfriend was a local Catholic boy of Italian descent and a few years older than I was. He had dropped out of school in his junior year. At that time, many working-class teens believed that an education wasn't necessary since they could easily work construction jobs or as sack boys at the grocery store. After all, many of their fathers hadn't graduated from school either and held perfectly good jobs, from which they would eventually retire with an adequate pension.

I often smiled as I pretended to be comfortable in the new role of girlfriend. I was now included in on most activities my boyfriend participated in, especially family gatherings. These get-togethers unnerved me because there was so much alcohol involved. Everyone drank; his parents, aunts, uncles, and friends, and he, too, usually had a can of beer in his hand. Sitting in the middle of their living room, I watched in silent terror as his mother poured herself glass after glass of vodka and began to slur her words and stumble over the furniture. His father remained impassive, as though this scene was repeated often. I knew my father also had a problem with alcohol, but in this woman's house there were bottles of vodka hidden in every nook and cranny—behind books and in every jacket in the closet. I wondered about the impact her drinking must have had on the three boys in the family, who did their best to both ignore her drinking and not attract attention to themselves.

Having a boyfriend was a unique experience for me. It felt different to go places with a boy rather than a girlfriend, especially when you didn't have to pay your way most times. I developed a somewhat misguided idea that this must be *the* relationship and was available at a moment's notice to go to movies or just cruising. We became engaged on graduation night in 1959, much to my parents' dismay. I wasn't ready and they knew it, but of course I didn't know it. I imagined him to be my knight, destined to whisk me away from it all. Reflecting on it today, the relationship was destined to fail from the beginning—and it did. After a few years of pretending to be someone

I wasn't, I ended up disillusioned and in shock to find this fantasy romance was in shambles. But that's a 1960s story.

In contrast, my parents were married for sixty-eight years. Since their relationship clearly wasn't perfect, I often wondered why they stayed together, and the only answer I have is that they loved each other in their own way. They had been born in an era when families stayed together, no matter the cost, even though their personalities were polar opposites.

Fortunately, once the children were all grown and out of the family home, the magic of art appeared in their lives. They slowly began to develop a cottage industry of traditional tinwork that was quite different from the work my father had done as a sheet-metal man in Los Alamos.

Dad was outgoing and friendly and loved to chat with strangers when they came to visit my parents in their kitchen studio. Mom was shy and quiet, intimidated by wealthy people, *los ricos*, smoothing her hair and the front of her apron as she concentrated on her work.

There was some precedent in our family for their success with tinwork. When my mother was a child in Ojo de la Vaca, a distant relative of the family, José Maria Apodaca, traveled to Santa Fe periodically to replenish his supply of discarded oil cans from which he crafted tin mirrors, sconces, and boxes at the turn of the century. While losing his eyesight, he taught Primo Patricio how to punch tin. Patricio learned to make solder from pitch resin gathered from the piñon trees and mixed it with oil to make flux to solder pieces together with the homemade soldering iron heated on the cast-iron stove. Both men traveled to Santa Fe and other villages to sell their wares. (Apodaca's tin creations from that era are highly sought after by collectors today.)

Mother was always doing something to occupy her time when she wasn't working with tin—taking an art class, learning how to do a different kind of embroidery. Mom never forgot our birthdays and made it a point to call, no matter where we were. I treasure some of the items she gave me, items she lovingly crafted by hand. She didn't care too much for sports or politics; those were subjects she rarely concerned herself with, except in the case of Nancy Lopez, the pro golfer from Roswell, New Mexico. Both Mother and Dad would watch her play on television while they crafted their tin items at their kitchen table, cheering her on to victory. Fiercely loyal to her culture, Mom just wanted this young Mexican girl to succeed.

She prayed every day, for all of us and for all our needs. I think it was prayer that kept her going. She wasn't afraid of anything: animals, insects, or people. Any time we talked about death, she said she wasn't afraid to die, that she was ready. Dad wasn't so sure. I always thought he would go down fighting to stay around until the very end.

As adults, when we wanted to take Mother out to eat or to a museum function, he would tell her, *"No te mandas sola"* (you don't boss yourself). She would then decide she'd better not go with us. Had Mother exhibited any independent notions, it would have invoked the wrath of the gods. "You're not going," meant just that. There was no valid reason for it, but that's the way it was. I recall bursting into laughter when Dad turned his back and Mother would scrunch up her face in a disapproving grimace and make hand gestures, bobbing her head back and forth like the puppet she must have felt she was. Dad was in control and that's the way he liked it.

In fact, in all the families in the neighborhood, the father ruled. No misbehavior ever got past him, and at one time or another, every one of the neighboring children experienced a whipping with The Belt, even some of the girls, and even in our family. We learned to be obedient early in our lives. "Wait 'til your father gets home" was a dreaded warning during childhood. And when we rebelled, just like my mother, we were told *"no se mandan solos"* (you don't boss yourselves), a reminder that our parents, and fathers in particular, held the keys to the kingdom and we'd better be on our best behavior.

It puzzled me that my grandmother's generation had a matriarchal culture in which the women set the rules of the household, and my father's generation was patriarchal, where the men established the rules. I questioned how one generation could

Emilio and Senaida Romero, doing tinwork in family kitchen.

reverse the system and wondered how our family dynamics would have been different had my dad not been such a staunch patriarch. I loved Grandma Romero, but she was a traditional matriarch who was the head of her household, and her word was the final say. She ruled and made the rules. She saved the money and determined how to spend it, even in matters involving real estate. Grandpa was the worker bee who took care of the basic needs. She often expressed the opinion that no other woman could tell my father what to do, so maybe that is why he and other men in our neighborhood became so patriarchal.

Whatever demons had plagued my father in the 1950s, after his retirement in late 1960, their art brought them into a new phase of their lives. They were responsible for reestablishing the art of the traditional tinsmith in northern New Mexico, gaining national recognition for their work and winning numerous awards in local art markets. In 1987 they were honored by the National Endowment for the Arts for excellence in the arts, receiving not only a monetary award but a certificate presented to them by President Ronald Reagan at the White House. My sister Rosalie fondly recalls referring to Mother as "Grandma

Moses" because she created her finest works in colcha stitch, the traditional stitchery of northern New Mexico, and tinwork when she was in her late sixties and early seventies. She continued to work at the craft until shortly before her death in 2001.

Postscript

Walking through the old Houghton Street neighborhood recently, I noticed most of the houses have been remodeled to some extent. Like the house I grew up in, some have new owners, but most of them are still owned by the same families.

All in all, of the children who grew up on West Houghton Street in the 1950s, almost all have had great successes in life. The cross-section of occupations includes sheet-metal men, contractors, mechanics, plumbers, accountants, bankers, real estate developers, mayoral candidates, flamenco dancers, guitarists, teachers, and artists. In my family alone, my parents lived to see the successes of seven artists: one sculptor, three tinsmiths, two *santeras*, and one business consultant–colcha stitcher to keep it altogether. The grandchildren of the neighborhood include graduates from Notre Dame, Stanford, UNM, and Georgetown, airline pilots, soldiers, legal secretaries, gift shop owners, retail clerks, contractors, roofers, engineers, artists, jewelers, singers, musicians, computer whizzes, and a bevy of other occupations.

Three of the Gonzales children are deceased, as are most of the Catanachs. Almost all of us have lost our parents. Still remaining are Uncle Rumaldo and Aunt Lena, Uncle Rudy and

The family home on West Houghton Street, present day.

Grandma Romero's house on West Houghton Street, present day.

Aunt Mary, and Uncle Willie, who never remarried after his wife's death in the 1960s. Uncle Rumaldo's house and the Martínez, Tapia, Gonzales, and Fresquez homes have been lovingly preserved, as have others in the neighborhood. Around the bend toward Galisteo Street many of the original homes still remain. Grandma Romero's house still stands, as a tribute to our beginnings on West Houghton Street, a reminder of growing up in the 1950s, and the tortillas that nourished our bodies, our hearts, and our souls.